Unix Unleashed: From Rookie Star in the World of Command Lines

Table of Contents

Chapter 1: Welcome to the Command Line Jungle

1. Welcome to the jungle, friend. You've just ventured into the wild world of Unix, a land of blinking cursors, mysterious commands, and the occasional random system error. Don't worry—it's not as terrifying as it sounds. In fact, the command line, though often painted as the villain in many computer horror stories, is really just a misunderstood friend. It's been there for decades, quietly running in the background, doing all the heavy lifting while most graphical user interfaces (GUIs) take the spotlight. But you're here now, and that's what matters. You've chosen the road less traveled, a road that requires precision, logic, and a healthy sense of humor. You'll get to know your terminal in ways that will make you appreciate its raw, no-nonsense power. A command line is like a magic wand— you just need to know the right spells. Unix, with its vast array of tools, is the wizard's toolkit. As we journey deeper into this wild jungle, you'll find that the trees are full of strange commands, the vines are pathways to power, and the occasional jaguar is just an unexpected bug you'll squash with ease.

2. Now, you may be wondering, "Why command line? Why not stick with the shiny, point-and-click GUI world?" Well, my friend, that's like asking why a Swiss Army knife is better than a regular spoon. Both are useful, but one is more flexible, versatile, and powerful. The command line allows you to do things faster, more efficiently, and—dare I say—more impressively. While clicking through menus can be satisfying, it's a bit like riding a tricycle through the jungle: it's cute, but it's slow. In contrast, mastering Unix is like jumping on a sleek, off-road bike that can handle any terrain. You'll be able to accomplish things in mere seconds that would take you minutes or hours with a GUI. Once you realize that you can manipulate your computer with just a few keystrokes, you'll wonder why you ever used a mouse at all. Plus, let's face it: typing commands feels pretty cool. It's like you're a wizard casting spells, but instead of wands, you're wielding terminal commands like `ls`, `cd`, and `grep`.

3. So, what exactly is Unix? It's an operating system, sure, but it's so much more than that. Unix is the granddaddy of most modern operating systems. It's the bedrock upon which Linux, macOS, and many other systems are built. Imagine it as a sturdy oak tree, its roots running deep into the tech world, and everything around it is just a branch of that great tree. It's known for its robustness, security, and multitasking prowess. But the best part? It's built on a philosophy of simplicity and clarity. Unlike some operating systems that try to do everything for you, Unix gives you the freedom to do things your own way. The command line is your personal toolset, a place where you can directly communicate with your computer. You'll get to work with files, directories, and processes, all with the power of your own fingertips. And while it may seem daunting at first, once you get the hang of it, you'll be surprised how intuitive it all becomes. Unix may not hold your hand, but it will make you feel like a superhero once you're comfortable with it.

4. The terminal is your portal into the Unix jungle, and it might look like a blank, intimidating black screen at first. Don't let that fool you. Underneath that simple interface lies an entire world of functionality and power. At its core, the terminal is just a place where you can type text and give your computer instructions. No need for fancy buttons or sliders—just you and the machine, communicating in a language of commands. If you've ever used a search engine, you're already familiar with the basics of interacting with a command line. In fact, typing commands into a terminal is a bit like asking Google questions, except your answers come in the form of system processes, files, and outputs. The cool part? You don't have to click on anything—everything you do is typed directly. It's like the digital equivalent of speaking directly to your computer. The more you learn, the more you'll appreciate the elegance and efficiency of this old-school interface.

5. But wait, where do you even begin? Don't worry. All you need is the terminal. On most Unix-based systems, you can open it with just a few clicks or keystrokes. In fact, the terminal is your doorway to everything Unix. If you've ever used a terminal emulator in Linux or macOS, you've already seen the magic. The blinking cursor is a bit like a friendly tap on the shoulder, saying, "Hey, what can I do for you today?" And that's where it starts. The terminal may look like a blank canvas, but once you start typing, you'll see that it's anything but empty. The `ls` command, for example, will list all the files in the current directory. Simple, right? Yet, with that one command, you've made contact with the deepest part of your computer's file system. It's like opening the door to a hidden world that's been there all along, waiting for you to discover it.

6. Let's talk about files for a moment. Files in Unix are much more than just little bundles of data. They're the backbone of the operating system. Every program, document, image, and video you interact with is stored in files. Unix treats everything—yes, EVERYTHING—as a file. Devices, directories, and even network connections are viewed as files. If this sounds like a mind-bending concept, don't worry, you'll get used to it. The file system in Unix is hierarchical, meaning that files are organized in a tree-like structure. Think of your computer as a huge library with countless books. Files are the books, directories are the shelves, and the root directory is the library's main entrance. When you're working in the terminal, you're navigating through this library, looking for specific books (or files) to read, modify, or manipulate.

7. Now that you've opened the terminal, it's time to introduce yourself. The first command you'll want to learn is `pwd`, which stands for "print working directory." It's a simple command that shows you where you are in the file system. Think of it as your GPS in the command line jungle. When you run `pwd`, the terminal will tell you your exact location. For example, it might say something like `/home/username/Documents`. This is your current directory, the folder where you're working. You can think of this as your current position in the vast, interconnected landscape of your file system. Understanding where you are is critical, especially when you start navigating through different directories. The command is so basic yet so powerful—it's like checking your map before setting off on an adventure.

8. Next up: navigating the file system. If you're a fan of exploration (and let's face it, who isn't?), you'll love how Unix lets you navigate its file system with ease. The command for moving between directories is `cd`, which stands for "change directory." This is your mode of transportation in the Unix world. Using `cd`, you can venture to any part of the file system. For example, `cd /home/username/Documents` will transport you straight to your Documents folder. Want to go up a level? Just type `cd ..` and you'll move one directory up. It's like taking a shortcut through the jungle by hopping over the branches. If you want to return to your home directory, simply type `cd ~`, and boom— you're back to where you started. It's simple, efficient, and gives you the power to explore the system like never before.

9. One of the coolest things about Unix is its power to let you automate tasks. Imagine being able to schedule your tasks so that your computer does things for you. This is where the `cron` system comes in. Cron is your personal assistant, available 24/7, waiting to execute tasks on a schedule you define. Want to back up your files every night at 2 a.m.? No problem. Want to send yourself a reminder to eat lunch every day at noon? Easy. Cron can handle that. You write a "cron job" that tells the system what task to perform and when. For example, you could set a cron job to clean up your temp files every Sunday. It's like having a personal butler, except this one never forgets, never sleeps, and doesn't need tips.

10. Unix is a lot like a puzzle, and each command you learn is a piece that helps you unlock new parts of the system. As you start putting these pieces together, you'll begin to see the big picture: an efficient, flexible system that lets you control your computer in ways you never thought possible. The more you practice, the faster you'll become. And soon, you'll be typing commands with such ease, it'll feel like second nature. But don't worry, you don't have to be a coding genius to get started. Unix is all about learning by doing. You'll make mistakes (we all do), and that's part of the process. But the beauty of Unix is that it's forgiving, and the more you try, the more you'll understand. Plus, it's pretty hard to break anything—you can always learn from your errors and fix them. So take a deep breath, crack your knuckles, and let's keep going.

11. As you venture deeper into the command line jungle, you'll find that there's a whole world of helpful tools and commands at your disposal. One of the best ways to learn Unix

is by using the `man` command. Think of `man` as your personal guidebook to Unix. The `man` command shows you the manual for any command you type into the terminal. Want to know how the `ls` command works? Just type `man ls`, and you'll get a full rundown of all the options and parameters you can use. It's like having an infinite library at your fingertips. This is one of the most powerful tools you'll have as you explore the Unix world. The `man` pages can be long, but they're packed with useful information that can help you become a master of the command line.

12. You might be wondering if there's a way to make your time in the terminal a bit more... stylish. Well, you're in luck. Unix has a great feature that lets you customize your prompt, the little text that appears when you're waiting for your next command. The default prompt might look like a boring `$`, but with a few simple tweaks, you can make it show your username, current directory, or even the time. It's like putting your personal touch on your command line workspace. For example, you could have your prompt display your username followed by the folder you're in, so you always know exactly where you are. Or, you could add colors to make things pop. Customizing your prompt is a small step, but it can make working in the terminal feel more like home.

13. The beauty of Unix lies not just in its tools, but in how those tools work together. Each command is like an individual musician in a band, and when you combine them, you create a symphony of efficiency. This is where piping comes into play. The pipe symbol (|) lets you take the output of one command and send it as input to another. Imagine you have a list of files, but you only want to see the ones that are written in Python. You could use the `grep` command to search through the list for `.py` files. This is where the magic of piping happens: you can take the output of `ls` and pipe it into `grep` to filter for Python files. It's like combining the best of both worlds: the power of individual commands and the elegance of their collaboration.

14. Once you get the hang of the basics, it's time to dive deeper into the inner workings of Unix. There's a whole universe of advanced commands and concepts to explore. You'll start learning about processes and how Unix multitasks. Processes are the lifeblood of your computer, running in the background to perform all sorts of tasks. You'll learn how to manage these processes, prioritize them, and even kill them when they misbehave. Understanding how processes work will help you become more efficient, and it'll give you the confidence to tackle more complex tasks. Don't worry—we'll get to that soon. For now, just remember that the journey to becoming a Unix rock star is paved with knowledge, patience, and a sense of humor.

15. So, here's the deal: mastering Unix isn't about memorizing every single command and option. It's about building a mental toolkit and learning how to solve problems efficiently. Over time, you'll start recognizing patterns, and before you know it, you'll be solving problems with ease. You'll be able to navigate your file system, automate tasks, monitor processes, and much more—all by typing a few simple commands. Unix isn't here to hold your hand, but once you understand its rhythm, you'll be dancing to its beat. You

won't just be a user—you'll be a creator. The jungle of Unix may seem dense at first, but with the right tools and mindset, you'll soon find yourself at the top of the food chain.

As you continue your journey through the command line jungle, you'll discover just how vast and deep the Unix ecosystem really is. There's no end to what you can achieve with Unix once you understand its core principles. Want to build a custom environment? Done. Want to automate repetitive tasks? No sweat. Need to check system performance? You've got the tools. As you get comfortable with basic commands and concepts, you'll be eager to explore more advanced topics, like process management, networking, and scripting. And with each step, your confidence will grow. What once seemed like a confusing tangle of commands will soon be a well-organized toolkit for conquering whatever challenges come your way. The beauty of Unix is that it's not just a static system—it's an ever-evolving adventure. You're not just learning an operating system; you're developing a set of problem-solving skills that will serve you in countless ways. You'll find that the more you know, the more you realize there's always something new to discover.

And here's the best part: Unix doesn't need to be learned in one sitting. This journey is about building blocks—one command, one concept, and one discovery at a time. Think of each new tool as a new piece of equipment in your digital survival kit. The more you gather, the more resourceful you become. It's a process of constant learning, of small wins that add up to big achievements. Don't worry if you don't get it all at once. The terminal might feel intimidating now, but every time you successfully execute a command, you're chipping away at that fear. You'll soon be navigating the Unix wilderness with confidence, understanding that each new challenge is just another opportunity to learn and grow. It's like hiking up a steep trail—you might get winded at times, but when you reach the top, you'll be amazed at the view.

Unix also has a sense of community that you'll soon appreciate. Unlike some systems that keep everything behind closed doors, Unix and its derivatives have open-source roots. This means that there's a massive community of users, developers, and enthusiasts out there sharing knowledge, tools, and advice. Need help? Chances are, someone has already encountered your problem and posted the solution online. Forums, mailing lists, and websites like Stack Overflow are treasures troves of wisdom. The Unix community thrives on collaboration, and once you get involved, you'll find that the command line isn't just an isolated experience—it's part of a global conversation. As you grow in your skills, you'll have the opportunity to give back, whether by answering questions, contributing to projects, or even writing your own tutorials. The sense of belonging to this larger community can make the Unix journey feel less lonely, and more like an exciting, shared expedition.

So, now that you've entered the jungle, you might be wondering what your next steps should be. First, embrace the small wins. Learn how to navigate directories, manipulate files, and run basic commands. These may seem like small tasks, but they're the foundation of everything that follows. The key to mastering Unix isn't about speed—it's about consistency. Spend time with each new concept until it clicks, and then move on to the next. With each step forward, you'll start to notice a shift: the command line will go from feeling like an intimidating black box to a friendly, efficient tool. The more you practice, the more second nature it will become. Trust the process. Like any adventure, it's about enjoying the journey, not just rushing to the destination. And as you progress, you'll find that Unix's simplicity is its greatest strength.

By now, you've taken your first steps into the world of Unix, and you've seen that while it may seem vast and complicated, it's also incredibly powerful and rewarding. The jungle might be full of twists and turns, but every turn leads to something new. Whether you're automating tasks, scripting your way to victory, or just exploring your file system, there's always something to discover. And remember, even the most seasoned Unix veterans were once in your shoes. They stumbled, they learned, and they grew. Soon enough, you'll be the one answering questions, sharing tips, and helping newcomers navigate the wilds of Unix. So, welcome to the jungle. It's going to be an exciting, rewarding ride. With the right mindset and a willingness to learn, you'll be rocking the command line before you know it. The adventure is just beginning!

Chapter 2: Hello, World! Your First Command

1. Congratulations! You've officially entered the realm of Unix, and the best way to celebrate this monumental achievement is by running your very first command. It's a rite of passage for every Unix user—a command so simple yet so powerful that it's been a tradition in the programming world for decades. It's time to say "Hello, World!" and begin your journey into the command line jungle. But here's the twist: unlike a typical greeting, this "Hello, World!" doesn't involve shaking hands or waving. Instead, it's just a few keystrokes that'll make the terminal speak back to you. You don't need a complex program to get started. No, today we'll keep it simple and let the machine show you what it's made of. And while it's a basic command, you'll quickly discover that every great journey begins with the simplest steps. So, let's dive in. All you need to do is type `echo "Hello, World!"` and press Enter. Bam! You've just executed your first Unix command. It's that easy—and that powerful.

2. The `echo` command is your first tool in the Unix toolkit, and you'll use it a lot. It might look like a simple command, but it has a hidden power—it displays whatever text you put after it. In this case, we asked it to display the words "Hello, World!"—and guess what? The terminal complied. This is what Unix is all about: giving instructions to your computer and watching it execute them without any unnecessary fluff. The beauty of Unix is that it doesn't try to hide its magic behind colorful icons or complex menus. Instead, it gives you the power to directly communicate with your system. The `echo` command doesn't just speak words; it opens the door to a world where your input creates results. It's a reminder that Unix is simple yet profound. In the same way that "Hello, World!" is a computer's first step into programming, it's your first step into becoming a Unix expert.

3. Let's break it down, shall we? The `echo` command is straightforward, but that doesn't mean we should skip over the details. When you type `echo "Hello, World!"`, you're telling the terminal, "Hey, I want you to *echo* these words back to me." The `echo` command then takes everything inside the quotes and prints it to the screen. But hold on —why quotes? Well, they're there to group the text together. If you left them out, Unix

would have trouble interpreting your sentence properly. Quotes help define boundaries, much like a fence around a garden. Without the fence, the garden (or, in this case, the text) could spread into places it doesn't belong. So, always remember to use quotes when you want Unix to handle multiple words as a single block of text. It's a small detail, but one that will make your life a whole lot easier.

4. Now, you might be wondering: why start with `echo`? Well, `echo` is the perfect command for beginners. It gives you immediate feedback and shows you that you're already interacting with the system. In Unix, feedback is everything. As you type commands and run them, the terminal responds, confirming that your instructions were understood (or letting you know where things went awry). This feedback loop helps you understand how your actions affect the system. The more you play with commands, the more you'll see how quickly the terminal responds. And trust us—this real-time interaction is addictive. Before long, you'll be typing commands like a seasoned pro, testing the limits of what you can do with Unix. So, don't underestimate the power of `echo`—it's your first window into this world, and it opens wide.

5. Speaking of feedback, let's talk about what you saw after running your command. When you typed `echo "Hello, World!"`, the terminal should have immediately displayed the phrase you entered. This is called output. In the world of Unix, output is the result of the command you just executed. Whether you're asking the system to show a file, run a process, or print a string of text, the result you get back is the output. For now, your output was just the string "Hello, World!"—simple, yet satisfying. Output is like the applause after a great performance. It tells you, "Yes, the command was executed successfully, and here's what you asked for." Every time you run a command and see the output, you're taking a step further into understanding how Unix operates.

6. The magic of the command line is that it's interactive. It's not like reading a book or watching a video—you actively engage with the system. Just like playing a game where every action leads to a new outcome, the terminal reacts instantly to what you type. This makes it a perfect environment for learning. Each time you run a command, you can see the immediate result. If something works, awesome! If not, you have a chance to figure out what went wrong. Think of the terminal as a training ground where every command you execute brings you closer to mastering Unix. Unlike other systems where you might click buttons and hope for the best, in Unix, you get to directly control the process. There's no guessing game here—it's all about precision and clarity.

7. Let's take this a step further. You've learned how to execute a command that outputs a simple string. But Unix is so much more than just printing text. In fact, everything in Unix revolves around files—files that contain data, programs, and system configurations. While `echo` might seem like a toy command, it's actually laying the foundation for more advanced operations. For example, instead of just printing "Hello, World!" to the screen, you could redirect that output to a file. By adding `> hello.txt` after your command, you would create a file called `hello.txt` and store the phrase "Hello, World!" inside it. That's right—you just saved something to your computer using just one simple

command. And guess what? You can open that file and see your text there. This is just the beginning of how Unix allows you to interact with files and data.

8.   You might be thinking, "Okay, that's neat, but I can just open a text editor and type something into a file." True. But here's where Unix shines—it allows you to do these things quickly and efficiently from the command line, without ever needing to open a GUI-based application. Imagine you're working on a project and you need to create multiple files with the same content. Instead of manually opening an editor for each one, you can use `echo` and redirection to create as many files as you need, each one with its own content. The speed at which you can manipulate files from the terminal is unrivaled. And this command is just the start. As you progress, you'll see how Unix lets you build powerful workflows using these simple tools.

9.   Another cool thing about the `echo` command is that it's customizable. You don't have to stick to just printing plain text. You can use escape sequences to format your output. For example, `echo -e "Hello, \nWorld!"` will print the word "Hello," followed by a new line, and then "World!" This means you can break up your text and even insert special characters, like tabs (`\t`) or other formatting symbols. It's like adding a touch of personality to your command output. As you explore more commands, you'll find that formatting plays a huge role in making your terminal interactions more effective. Whether it's adding colors, new lines, or even special symbols, Unix gives you the flexibility to control how information is displayed.

10. Don't get too comfortable yet! The `echo` command is an important tool, but there's a lot more to discover. You might think you've learned all there is to know from this one command, but Unix always has something new to teach you. For example, you can use `echo` to check environment variables—those little pieces of information that store configuration settings for your session. For instance, try typing `echo $HOME` to find out the path to your home directory. This is just a sneak peek into the world of environment variables, which will become your best friends as you start customizing your Unix environment. With `echo`, you've already learned how to interact with your system's variables and configure things to suit your needs.

11. The best part about learning `echo` is that it lays the groundwork for understanding how Unix commands are built and how they work together. Unix commands are often modular —each one does one thing, but does it really well. When you combine these simple commands, you can perform complex operations. Think of it like cooking: each ingredient is basic on its own, but when combined, they create something extraordinary. In the same way, commands like `echo` become building blocks that allow you to do incredible things. Over time, you'll learn how to string commands together to automate tasks, manipulate files, and interact with your system in powerful ways. The world of Unix commands is vast, and `echo` is your first step into exploring it.

12. If you're thinking, "Okay, I get it—`echo` is useful, but is this all Unix can do?" Oh, my friend, you have only just begun. The beauty of Unix lies in the sheer variety and

versatility of its commands. From file manipulation to process management, from networking to security, there's virtually no limit to what you can do once you've mastered the basics. As you continue your journey, you'll encounter new commands and techniques that will make you more efficient, more powerful, and—most importantly—more confident in using your system. But all great journeys start with a single step, and `echo` is yours.

13. As with all things in life, the key to mastery is practice. You won't become a Unix wizard overnight, but every command you run, no matter how small, adds to your skill set. So, take your time with `echo`. Experiment with different text formats, explore how you can redirect output to files, and see how the command interacts with variables. Play around with the options and see what happens. The more you tinker, the more you'll understand the inner workings of Unix—and the more fun you'll have. Unix might seem like a jungle at first, but once you get comfortable, it becomes a second home.

14. One thing you'll notice as you progress is that Unix commands often come with a wealth of options and parameters. `echo` has a few options of its own, like `-n`, which prevents it from adding a new line at the end of the output. Want to get fancy? Try `echo -n "Hello, World!"`—notice the lack of a line break. This small change can make a big difference in how your output is formatted. Don't worry if you don't understand all the options at first. Just know that as you grow more comfortable, you'll start to see patterns. Soon, you'll be able to guess what certain options do and use them to make your commands more powerful.

15. You've now seen just how simple and powerful the command line can be. And this is just the beginning. You've learned how to interact with your system using one basic command, but you've also learned an important lesson: Unix is all about precision and flexibility. Every command is a tool in your toolbox, and with each new command, your ability to shape the system becomes greater. So, as you move forward, remember this: mastering Unix isn't about memorizing commands—it's about understanding how each one works, experimenting, and building your skills over time. Your next challenge awaits, and it's going to be a fun ride.

As we wrap up this chapter, let's take a moment to appreciate just how much you've already achieved. You've taken your first step into the command line world with `echo`, and that's something to be proud of. While it may seem small now, the foundation you're building is going to serve you in powerful ways. Unix may not always be easy, but it's a place where every step forward feels rewarding, and that sense of accomplishment is what makes it so exciting. You've now learned to interact with your terminal, produce output, and manipulate that output in new ways. The best part is that you're just scratching the surface. The more you experiment, the more you'll discover, and before long, you'll be solving problems and automating tasks that used to seem impossible. Think of each new command as a new tool in your belt, and with each tool, you'll build your expertise and confidence.

But don't get ahead of yourself—there's no rush. This journey is about steady progress, and every command you learn brings you closer to mastering the art of Unix. The beauty of the command line lies in its simplicity, but also in its depth. What seems simple now will evolve as you become more familiar with the nuances of Unix. Soon, you'll be crafting your own commands, chaining them together, and using them to automate your tasks. As you explore deeper into the world of Unix, you'll begin to understand how each command, no matter how small, contributes to the larger ecosystem of the operating system. You'll realize that mastering the command line is less about memorizing specific commands and more about building a mindset — a mindset that is confident, flexible, and always eager to learn.

Remember that the key to mastering Unix isn't just about getting the commands right — it's about getting comfortable with the process of experimentation and learning. Unix rewards curiosity. If something doesn't work the first time, it's not the end of the world. It's just part of the process. Learn from it, try again, and remember that each mistake is a lesson in disguise. With Unix, you won't be learning in a vacuum. Every time you run a command, it's a chance to see the system in action, and that kind of feedback helps solidify your understanding. So embrace the trial-and-error nature of learning, and don't shy away from experimenting with new commands. The more you interact with the system, the more you'll uncover.

Now, let's briefly talk about one more thing before we wrap up: documentation. Unix is an incredibly well-documented system, and that's a huge advantage for you as a learner. Whenever you're unsure about a command or its options, don't hesitate to pull up the manual. The `man` command is your best friend here. By typing `man echo`, for example, you can see the full documentation for the `echo` command, including all the options you can use. This documentation is detailed, reliable, and available at your fingertips. As you encounter new commands, the manual will be your guide, helping you understand what each command does and how it fits into the larger Unix ecosystem. Think of it as your digital map through the jungle of Unix. With the `man` command, you'll never feel lost for long.

By now, you've already seen how a simple command like `echo` can open up a whole new world of possibilities. You've learned how to use it, how to manipulate its output, and how to redirect that output to files. These foundational skills will be the building blocks for more complex commands and tasks in the future. As you move forward in your Unix journey, remember that each new skill will stack on top of the last. Unix isn't about learning one command and calling it a day — it's about constantly building and refining your skillset. Each new chapter will introduce you to new tools, new ways of thinking, and new problems to solve. With each step, you'll gain more control over your computer and become more comfortable in the command line environment. And that, my friend, is what will make you a Unix rockstar. So, take a deep breath, pat yourself on the back for completing your first command, and get ready for the next adventure. The journey has only just begun!

Chapter 3: File System Fundamentals: Not As Boring As It Sounds

1.   Welcome to the heart of Unix: the file system. It may not sound exciting at first, but trust me, understanding the file system is like learning the map of a treasure island — everything you do in Unix revolves around it. Whether you're opening a document, running a program, or even browsing the web, everything on your computer is stored in

the file system. The file system is where all the data is stored, organized, and accessed. You can think of it as the filing cabinet of your computer, but with far more style and a bit of magic thrown in. The real beauty of Unix's file system is how it treats everything as a file—directories, devices, and even processes. Yes, you heard me right—processes are files too. It's like a movie where every character is an important part of the plot. So, let's dive into this fascinating world and see what makes Unix's file system tick. The good news is, once you understand it, you'll be navigating Unix like a pro in no time.

2. To begin, let's start with the very top of the tree—the root directory. In Unix, all paths begin with a single slash (`/`), which represents the root directory. It's the parent of everything else, the mother of all directories, and the starting point for all file paths. Think of it as the trunk of the tree. Everything else branches out from here. Unlike Windows, which uses drive letters like `C:` or `D:`, Unix has a single unified file system. This makes navigating a Unix system both simpler and more powerful, since every file or directory has a unique path that starts from the root. You'll never get lost in a maze of different drives and partitions. The root directory is the foundation upon which everything else is built—whether it's your home directory, system files, or external devices, they all have paths that trace back to the root.

3. So, where do you live in the Unix world? Well, that would be your home directory. Your home directory is like your digital living room—your personal space, where your files, documents, and projects hang out. In Unix, your home directory is usually represented as `~`, a tilde symbol. For example, if your username is `john`, your home directory will be `/home/john`. This is where you start out when you log in and where all your personal files are kept. Whenever you're in doubt, just remember that `~` always refers to your home directory. It's your safe zone, the place where your files are easy to access and organize. You can navigate there with just `cd ~`, and from there, you're free to explore and create. It's a personal space, and you can set it up however you want, much like decorating your own room.

4. As you explore the file system, you'll encounter directories. A directory is simply a container for files, and just like folders in your computer's GUI, directories help you organize your files into neat categories. Directories can contain both files and other directories—yes, directories can have children. This hierarchical structure is what makes the Unix file system so powerful. It's like a family tree for your files: every file or directory has a parent and a location, making it easy to keep everything in order. For example, you might have a directory called `Documents`, inside which you have multiple subdirectories like `Work` and `Personal`. Each of those subdirectories can hold more files and directories, creating a nested structure. The more you work with directories, the more you'll appreciate how they keep your system organized and efficient. A neat system is an efficient system, and that's what Unix does best.

5. Speaking of directories, let's talk about the command used to list them: `ls`. This simple command is one of the most important tools in your Unix toolbox. It stands for "list," and it shows you the contents of a directory. When you run `ls` in your current directory, it

displays all the files and directories contained within. But don't let its simplicity fool you — `ls` is capable of doing some pretty cool things. Add the `-l` option, like so: `ls -l`, and you'll get more detailed information, such as file permissions, file sizes, and modification dates. Add `-a` to see hidden files (those starting with a dot, like `.bashrc`). These hidden files are often configuration files for your system and your shell, but don't worry—you'll get to know them soon. The `ls` command is your go-to way to peek inside a directory, and it's your first step in exploring the vast file system.

6. Now, what about moving around in this jungle of directories? That's where the `cd` command comes in. `cd` stands for "change directory," and it's your method of transportation in the file system. When you run `cd`, you can move between directories with ease. Want to visit your `Documents` directory? Just type `cd Documents` and hit Enter. You can also use `cd ..` to move up one level in the directory tree. Think of `..` as the "parent" directory—it takes you one level higher. If you want to go directly to your home directory, just type `cd ~`, and boom, you're back home. Navigating directories is like walking down a trail in the woods, with `cd` being your trusty compass. The more familiar you become with the structure, the easier it will be to get to where you want to go.

7. So, now you know how to list and navigate directories, but what about creating and removing them? This is where the `mkdir` and `rmdir` commands come in. `mkdir`, which stands for "make directory," allows you to create a new directory wherever you are in the file system. Let's say you want to create a directory called `Projects` in your home directory. Simply type `mkdir Projects`, and voila—a new directory appears. If you want to remove a directory, use `rmdir`. However, keep in mind that `rmdir` can only remove empty directories. If you try to delete a directory that contains files, you'll need to first remove its contents. Don't worry—there are ways to remove directories that aren't empty, but that's a bit more advanced, so we'll get to that later. For now, just remember that `mkdir` is your key to building new folders, and `rmdir` is your tool for cleaning up after yourself.

8. Now that you're familiar with creating directories, let's talk about files—the real heart of the file system. Files are where data is stored, and there are many types of files: text files, image files, executable files, and much more. You can create a file in Unix with a simple command like `touch filename.txt`. The `touch` command creates an empty file with the name you specify. If you try to open the file afterward, you'll see that it's blank, just waiting for data to be written into it. You can then use editors like `nano` or `vim` to add text to the file. While creating files with `touch` is easy, you'll soon discover that files in Unix are much more than just containers for text. You can use them to store scripts, system configurations, and much more.

9. Files are also associated with something called permissions. Permissions control who can read, write, and execute a file. These permissions are crucial for securing your system and making sure the right people (or programs) can access the right files. In Unix, there are

three basic types of permissions: `r` for read, `w` for write, and `x` for execute. Each file or directory has a set of permissions associated with it, and these permissions are divided into three categories: the owner (you), the group (other users in your group), and others (everyone else). For example, you might see something like `-rw-r--r--` when listing files with `ls -l`. This means that the file is readable and writable by the owner, readable by the group, and readable by everyone else. Managing permissions is a fundamental part of working with Unix, and as you progress, you'll learn how to change and set permissions to fit your needs.

10. One of the most powerful aspects of the Unix file system is its use of symbolic links. A symbolic link, or symlink, is a special type of file that points to another file or directory. Think of it as a shortcut, but more flexible. You can create a symlink with the `ln -s` command, followed by the target file and the symlink name. For example, `ln -s /home/john/Documents /home/john/DocsShortcut` would create a shortcut to the `Documents` directory in your home folder, named `DocsShortcut`. You can use symlinks to organize files across directories, create backup shortcuts, or even link to files in other locations. Symlinks make working with the file system more efficient, and once you get used to them, they'll become a valuable tool in your Unix toolkit.

11. As you get more comfortable with Unix, you'll notice that the file system isn't just about directories and files—it's also about managing the data within them. Files are stored on disks, and Unix has several tools for monitoring disk usage. The `df` command shows how much disk space is being used and how much is available. If you're running low on space, `df` will let you know, helping you keep track of your system's health. You can also use `du` to check the space usage of individual files and directories. This is especially helpful when you need to clean up your system and free up space. Being able to monitor disk usage will make you a more effective Unix user, ensuring that your system doesn't become bloated with unnecessary files.

12. The beauty of Unix lies in its simplicity and flexibility. You can create, modify, and delete files and directories with just a few commands. But as you'll soon discover, the real power of Unix comes from its ability to chain these simple commands together. As you progress, you'll learn how to combine commands in creative ways, using pipes and redirection to process and manage your files more efficiently. For example, you might want to list all the files in a directory and then search for a specific pattern. With Unix, you can do that in a single line by piping the output of one command into another. This flexibility is one of the reasons Unix is so powerful—it gives you the tools to solve complex problems with just a few lines of code.

13. As we wrap up this chapter, it's important to remember that the file system is the backbone of Unix. Everything you do—whether it's creating files, navigating directories, or managing system resources—depends on how well you understand the file system. The better you understand the structure and organization of files, the more efficient you'll become at navigating and managing your system. So, practice the commands you've

learned, experiment with different file types, and get comfortable moving around the file system. With each step, you'll grow more confident in your Unix skills, and soon enough, the file system will feel like second nature.

As you continue to explore, one of the most powerful things about Unix's file system is its ability to handle large volumes of files efficiently. As you start to work with more files, you'll realize that keeping track of them becomes a challenge. Unix has some excellent tools to help you with this. For example, `find` is an incredibly useful command that allows you to search for files based on various criteria like name, size, type, or modification time. Want to find all `.txt` files in your home directory? Just run `find ~ -name "*.txt"`. This is a real game-changer, especially when you're managing large projects or need to locate something hidden deep within the file system. And let's not forget `locate`, which is even faster than `find` because it searches an indexed database of file names. It's like having your own personal librarian for the file system—everything at your fingertips, no matter how deep in the jungle you've gone.

And just when you think you've got everything figured out, Unix throws in another twist: file system mounting. You see, in Unix, external devices like USB drives, CDs, and network storage aren't just plugged into some random location on your system. No, they are *mounted* into the file system at specific points. This means that when you plug in a USB drive, for example, you're essentially creating a new branch on your file system tree. To access it, you have to mount it. The `mount` command is what connects these external devices to your file system. Want to mount a USB drive? You'd type something like `sudo mount /dev/sdb1 /mnt/usb`. Once it's mounted, you can interact with it just like any other directory. It's this mounting system that allows Unix to be so flexible and scalable, giving you the ability to add and remove storage devices seamlessly. It's like magic, except it's all happening in plain sight.

Another aspect of the Unix file system that may seem trivial at first but is extremely useful is the concept of symbolic links (symlinks). These are essentially shortcuts to other files or directories on your system. You've already seen symlinks in action, but let's take a deeper dive. Symlinks are like bookmarks in a book—they don't contain the information themselves but point you to where the information actually resides. This means you can have multiple ways to access the same file or directory, and the best part is that symlinks can point to files across different locations, even on different disks. Using symlinks in your projects or when organizing your data is a great way to make complex directory structures more navigable. Want to create a symlink to your music folder in a different directory? Just use `ln -s /path/to/music /path/to/shortcut/music` and there you have it—a shortcut that behaves just like the original.

With all these features and commands at your disposal, you'll quickly find that Unix gives you an incredible amount of control over your system. It's not just about organizing your files, it's about fine-tuning your environment to suit your needs. For example, you might want to change the default behavior of some of your commands or create aliases to make things faster. If you frequently use `ls -l`, why not create an alias like `alias ll="ls -l"` to save yourself a few keystrokes? You'll find that once you start customizing your environment, Unix becomes an incredibly personal system—tailored exactly to how you work. This level of customization is one of the reasons Unix has such a devoted following. The flexibility to make the system your own can turn an otherwise bland environment into a powerhouse of productivity.

And if you ever find yourself needing to perform more advanced file system management, don't worry—Unix has your back. There are powerful commands for checking the health of your file system, such as `fsck` (file system check). If your system ever starts acting up and you suspect file system corruption, `fsck` can help repair it. Similarly, if you're worried about running out of space, the `du` command (disk usage) can give you a detailed look at how much space your directories and files are using. These tools give you the ability to keep your system running smoothly, and they'll be invaluable when you start to manage more complex file systems or storage configurations.

As we come to the end of this chapter, it's important to remember that the Unix file system isn't just something you need to understand for practical purposes—it's also a mindset. When you're working with Unix, you're constantly thinking in terms of organization and structure. Each file and directory serves a purpose, and knowing how to manipulate them with precision makes you more efficient. The file system is the backbone of your Unix experience—it's the foundation upon which everything else is built. As you continue to explore, you'll learn to appreciate the elegance and power of the file system. The more familiar you become with it, the faster and more effectively you'll be able to accomplish your tasks.

To wrap things up, take a moment to practice the commands you've learned so far. Create directories, list files, change permissions, and experiment with symlinks. Explore the structure of your own file system, and get comfortable with navigating and manipulating files. The more you practice, the more intuitive it will become. Unix isn't about memorizing a set of rules; it's about developing a deep understanding of how the system works and using that knowledge to solve problems. Each chapter will build upon the last, and by the time you reach the more advanced concepts, you'll find that the Unix file system feels like second nature. So, keep experimenting, keep exploring, and keep building your knowledge. The adventure is far from over, and there's so much more to discover in the world of Unix.

Chapter 4: Navigating the Command Line: It's Like a Map, But Cooler

1. Picture this: You're standing at the entrance of a dense, sprawling jungle—an unknown land full of paths, treasures, and potential hazards. How do you navigate your way through? Well, just like a seasoned explorer, you need a map. In the world of Unix, the command line is your map, and navigating it properly is key to getting where you need to go. But unlike a traditional map, your command line isn't static—it's interactive and dynamic. Every command you type moves you through this landscape, each step taking you deeper into the heart of your system. If you've used a file explorer before, you're probably familiar with clicking around to browse directories and open files. In the Unix world, you'll navigate by typing commands instead of clicking. It's fast, it's efficient, and with a little practice, it'll feel like second nature. So let's roll up our sleeves and take a stroll through this digital jungle, where the trees are directories, and the paths are just a few keystrokes away.

2.	Before we start moving around, let's first talk about the layout of your Unix system. At the top of the hierarchy is the root directory, denoted by a single slash (`/`). Think of the root directory like the trunk of a tree. From here, everything branches out into various directories, each with its own set of files and subdirectories. Your home directory (`/home/username`) is one of these branches, and it's where all your personal files live. But the system also contains directories for system files, applications, and configurations. If you were to look at the entire system as a big tree, directories are the branches, and files are the leaves. You're going to spend a lot of time exploring these branches, so it's important to get a feel for how they're organized. And just like a jungle, the structure can be a bit confusing at first. But don't worry, with the right tools, navigating it will become a breeze.

3.	The command line interface is powerful, but it relies on you understanding how to get around. Luckily, there's no need to worry about street signs or traffic jams here—Unix has built-in commands that act as your navigation tools. The first tool in your arsenal is `pwd`, which stands for "print working directory." This command is your GPS—it tells you exactly where you are in the file system. When you open the terminal, you're initially placed in your home directory, but as you move around, you'll need to check your location. Simply type `pwd`, and the terminal will show you your current directory. For example, it might say `/home/john`. This is an invaluable tool for understanding where you are, especially when you start jumping around between directories. No need to guess where you are—you've got your very own digital compass.

4.	So, how do you move around the Unix jungle? Well, that's where the `cd` command comes in. `cd` stands for "change directory," and it's the primary tool for getting from one place to another. Need to move from your home directory to your Documents folder? Simple: type `cd Documents` and hit Enter. You're now in the Documents folder. Want to go back to your home directory? Just type `cd ~` and boom, you're back where you started. If you want to move up one level in the directory hierarchy, use `cd ..`. This is like stepping back to take a broader view of the landscape. If you're not sure where you are, you can always use `pwd` to check your location and confirm that you're on the right path. With `cd` and `pwd`, you've got the tools to confidently navigate your way through the file system like a pro.

5.	While `cd` is a great tool for getting from one directory to another, sometimes you'll want to see what's around you before you move. That's where `ls` comes in. `ls` stands for "list," and it shows you all the files and directories in your current location. When you run `ls`, it will display the names of all files and directories in your current directory, giving you a lay of the land. But the power of `ls` doesn't end there. You can add options to make it even more useful. For example, `ls -l` gives you a detailed listing, showing file sizes, permissions, and modification dates. Want to see hidden files? Use `ls -a` to display all files, including those that start with a dot (`.`), which are usually hidden from regular views. The more you get to know `ls`, the more you'll appreciate how it helps you survey your surroundings and figure out where to go next.

6. So far, you've learned how to move around and how to see what's in each directory. But what happens when you need to backtrack, or retrace your steps? That's where `cd` comes in handy again. Let's say you've been wandering around and find yourself deep in the jungle—maybe you've moved into a subdirectory and now need to return to a higher level. If you type `cd ..`, you'll move up one level. But what if you need to go back multiple levels at once? Easy—just type `cd ../../` to move up two levels. You can chain these commands together to go even higher: `cd ../../..` will take you up three levels. This is like having a helicopter that can lift you up through the canopy to get a better view of where you are. The ability to navigate quickly between levels of directories is crucial as you start working with more complex file systems.

7. Now, what happens when you want to go somewhere specific, like a completely different directory on the other side of the file system? Let's say you're in `/home/john/Downloads` and need to get to `/usr/local/bin`—but you're not sure exactly how to get there by jumping around between directories. That's where absolute paths come into play. An absolute path is a full, unambiguous address that tells you exactly where to go, starting from the root directory. To get to `/usr/local/bin`, you'd simply type `cd /usr/local/bin`, and no matter where you are in the system, it will take you straight to your destination. Absolute paths are incredibly useful when you need to jump to a specific location and don't want to mess around with relative paths. You can always count on absolute paths to take you directly to where you need to go, like a GPS with no room for error.

8. On the other hand, sometimes you want to navigate relative to where you already are, rather than specifying an absolute path. This is where relative paths come in. A relative path specifies the location of a file or directory in relation to your current position in the file system. For example, if you're in `/home/john` and want to go to the `Documents` directory, you don't need to type the full path like `/home/john/Documents`. Instead, you can just type `cd Documents`. The command assumes you want to go to `Documents` from your current location. Relative paths are more flexible because they allow you to move around without constantly needing to specify the full address. As you get more familiar with the file system, you'll find that relative paths are often quicker and easier to use.

9. Now, let's get a bit more adventurous. Sometimes, you'll find yourself in situations where you need to move around using wildcards—special characters that represent multiple files or directories at once. Wildcards are incredibly useful when you're working with many files or directories and don't want to type them all out individually. For example, the asterisk (`*`) is a wildcard that matches any number of characters. So, if you want to list all `.txt` files in your directory, just type `ls *.txt`. This will match any file that ends with `.txt`, regardless of what comes before it. Similarly, the question mark (`?`) matches

a single character, which can be useful if you know part of the name but not the full filename. Wildcards can save you time and effort, especially when you need to search for or interact with many files at once.

10. While navigating directories and using wildcards can make your journey through the file system easier, one of the most important skills is knowing how to manage and organize your files effectively. As you start to work with files more, you'll need to create, move, rename, and delete them. To create a new directory, you can use the `mkdir` command, and to remove an empty directory, `rmdir` is your tool of choice. Want to move a file or directory to a new location? Use `mv`, and if you need to rename a file, `mv` will work for that too. To delete files, `rm` is the command to use, but be careful—there's no trash can in Unix, so when you delete a file, it's gone for good (unless you're in a very specific setup). Mastering these commands will allow you to organize and maintain your file system like a true explorer.

11. As you continue to explore the command line, one of the things you'll start to appreciate is the power of customization. The way your command prompt looks, the colors of your directories, and even the behavior of certain commands can all be adjusted to fit your preferences. For instance, you can change the appearance of your command prompt by modifying the `.bashrc` file in your home directory. Want to make your prompt more informative by showing your current directory or time? It's all possible with a little customization. This level of flexibility is one of the things that makes Unix such a joy to work with—it's not just a system you use; it's a system you shape and mold to fit your needs.

12. As you get deeper into the world of Unix, you'll begin to rely less on the built-in file managers or graphical interfaces and more on your own ability to navigate quickly and efficiently. The command line may seem daunting at first, but once you get the hang of it, you'll find it's far faster and more powerful than anything a GUI can offer. You'll move with ease between directories, list and manipulate files, and quickly locate the exact file or program you need with just a few commands. You'll no longer feel like you're wandering aimlessly in the jungle; instead, you'll be confidently charting your own path.

13. So, take a deep breath, stretch your fingers, and keep practicing. The more you explore the command line, the more natural it will feel. With the right tools at your disposal, you'll soon be able to navigate any file system, no matter how complex. Unix may be a vast wilderness, but with a little knowledge of the terrain, you'll be able to navigate it like a seasoned pro. And remember, the more you practice, the better you'll get at reading your system's map—and the more confident you'll be as you continue your Unix journey. So go ahead—take your first steps, chart your path, and explore the digital jungle!

As we continue our exploration, let's take a moment to appreciate just how powerful the command line really is. It's more than just a way to move around—it's a tool that opens up a world of efficiency and customization. You might think that navigating a file system would be cumbersome, but in reality, Unix allows you to move faster, automate your processes, and work smarter. For instance, when you're moving multiple files around, rather than dragging and dropping them one by one in a graphical file manager, you can use commands like mv to move entire directories with a single line of text. It's like using a magic spell to complete a task in an instant. Want to copy files instead of moving them? Use cp, and you can create copies of files or directories quickly, without leaving your command line environment. Each of these commands can be used in combination to create powerful workflows that save you time and effort.

But perhaps the most important tool for navigating Unix is the combination of commands and options. Unix doesn't give you one-size-fits-all solutions; instead, it gives you a wide range of commands and options, all of which can be mixed and matched to suit your needs. For example, if you want to see a detailed list of files but also want to include hidden files, you can combine ls -la. The options -l and -a can be used together, giving you a detailed listing that includes files starting with a dot. Similarly, when navigating directories, you can use combinations of cd, ls, and pwd to quickly figure out where you are, what's in your directory, and what needs to be done. This flexibility means that as you become more comfortable with Unix, you'll be able to craft solutions to almost any problem with a few carefully chosen commands.

Now, you might be thinking, "But what if I don't know the exact name of the file or directory I want to navigate to?" No problem! This is where wildcards come in. Wildcards are your shortcut for working with files whose exact names you might not know, or when you want to match a pattern across multiple files. The most common wildcard is the asterisk (*), which matches any number of characters. For example, if you want to list all files that start with the word "project," you could use ls project*. This will show you every file in the directory whose name begins with "project," whether it's project1.txt, project_report.pdf, or project_notes.doc. Similarly, you can use the question mark (?) to match a single character. These wildcards save you from typing out long filenames or having to guess at the exact name of a file.

Sometimes, you might find yourself needing to work with files or directories across multiple locations in the file system, or even on different systems. This is where the power of paths comes into play. Unix gives you the ability to specify exactly where a file is located using paths. So far, you've been working with relative paths and absolute paths, but there's also the concept of a "home-relative path." The tilde (~) symbol represents your home directory, and you can use it to easily navigate there from anywhere in the file system. For example, if you're currently in /home/john/Documents and want to move to /home/john/Downloads, you can simply type cd ~/Downloads. The tilde acts as a shortcut to your home directory, making it easy to move between directories within your home directory without needing to type out the full path.

Another tool in your navigation toolkit is tab completion, which is your secret weapon for speeding up the process of typing long directory or file names. If you start typing part of a file or directory name and hit the Tab key, the terminal will automatically fill in the rest of the name for you (if there's only one match). This can save you a lot of time, especially when dealing with long and complex file names or directory structures. If there are multiple possible completions, you can press `Tab` twice, and the terminal will show you a list of options to choose from. It's like having a highly efficient co-pilot that fills in the gaps for you, making your navigation that much quicker.

One of the challenges in navigating large file systems is knowing which files are where and how to organize them. As you start working with more files and directories, you may find that your system becomes cluttered, and you need to clean things up. This is where commands like `find` become essential. `find` allows you to search for files based on specific criteria, such as their name, size, type, or modification time. For example, if you want to find all `.txt` files in your home directory, you could use `find ~ -name "*.txt"`. You can also use `find` to search by modification date, file permissions, and much more. This is incredibly useful when you have a large number of files and need to locate specific ones, or when you want to perform operations like deleting or moving files based on certain criteria.

As you progress in your Unix journey, you'll discover that efficient navigation isn't just about moving from one file or directory to another. It's also about knowing how to manage your environment and adapt your workflow. For example, the `history` command allows you to review the commands you've typed in the past, which is a great way to repeat common tasks or troubleshoot previous mistakes. You can even rerun a specific command from your history by typing `!number`, where `number` is the number of the command in the history list. This can save you a ton of time, especially if you frequently find yourself typing long or complex commands. The history command, combined with other tools like aliases (which allow you to create custom shortcuts for your favorite commands), makes Unix a more efficient and personalized system.

Now that you have the basic tools for navigation and file management, it's time to start thinking about how to combine these tools into powerful workflows. For example, you might want to list all the `.txt` files in your directory and then move them to a different folder. You can combine the `ls` and `mv` commands in a pipeline to do this. Or, perhaps you want to search for a particular pattern in a file and then redirect the output to a new file. By chaining commands together with pipes (`|`) and redirection (`>`), you can create efficient workflows that automate tedious tasks and make your Unix experience that much more powerful.

As you continue to experiment with these commands, you'll start to see the beauty of Unix's command-line interface. It's not just a place to run commands—it's a place where you can craft complex, customized solutions to almost any task. The key is understanding the tools available to you, how they work together, and how to adapt them to your needs. The more you practice, the more comfortable you'll become with navigating the system, and soon enough, the command line will feel like second nature.

It's important to remember that navigating the command line is not a race—it's about steady improvement. The more you familiarize yourself with the layout of your system and the commands at your disposal, the more confident you'll feel. Unix may seem like a dense jungle at first, but with the right tools and mindset, you'll soon find yourself gliding through it like a seasoned explorer. Take your time to practice, experiment, and learn, and soon you'll find that navigating the Unix system is not just efficient—it's downright fun.

As you continue to grow in your Unix proficiency, you'll find that the command line is not just a tool for getting things done, but an environment where you can truly become the master of your system. No more wasting time clicking through menus or feeling limited by GUI-based systems. In the world of Unix, you're in control, and the more you learn, the more you'll realize how powerful this control can be. So, take the time to explore, experiment, and make your way through the file system. Each step will bring you closer to mastering the command line and unlocking the full potential of your Unix environment.

The road ahead is full of opportunities. The more you familiarize yourself with the commands and tools at your disposal, the more efficient and powerful your workflow will become. Navigation is just the first step—once you're comfortable with the terrain, you'll be able to tackle more complex tasks with ease. Keep practicing, keep exploring, and before you know it, you'll be navigating the Unix jungle like a pro. The command line is your map, and with each new discovery, you'll unlock a world of possibilities!

Chapter 5: The Power of Permissions: Stop and Ask Yourself, "Who Am I?"

1. You've made it this far into the Unix world, exploring the command line jungle, learning to navigate directories, and manipulating files. But now, it's time to discuss something fundamental—something that will help you take full control over your files and your system: **permissions**. At its core, permissions in Unix are about control—who can read, write, and execute a file or directory. It's like a fortress where only the right people have access. Understanding how permissions work is crucial, not just for security, but for ensuring that your system runs smoothly. Imagine this scenario: You're working on a project, but suddenly you realize that you can't access a file you need. What happened? The file might be locked behind permission settings that don't allow you to read or modify it. This chapter will take you deep into the world of permissions, and by the end, you'll be able to wield them with ease, keeping your files secure and your system running like a well-oiled machine.

2. To understand Unix permissions, you first need to know **who** is interacting with your files. Unix is built on a multi-user model, which means multiple users can access and interact with the same system at the same time. Each user has a **user ID** (UID) and belongs to one or more **groups**. The **user** is the person who owns a file, while the **group** is a collection of users who are granted access to the file based on shared permissions. And then there's **everyone else**, a catch-all category that refers to all users who aren't the owner or part of the group. So, when it comes to permissions, you need to think in terms of three main categories: **owner**, **group**, and **others**. This structure ensures that only the appropriate people have access to your files, and you get to decide who gets to do what with them.

3. Let's break down how Unix represents permissions. When you list the files in a directory with `ls -l`, you'll notice a string of characters at the beginning of each line, like this:

-rwxr-xr--. This is the **permission string**, and it's made up of 10 characters. Here's what each character means:

- o The first character represents the file type: a dash (–) means it's a regular file, while a **d** means it's a directory.

- o The next three characters represent the **owner**'s permissions.

- o The following three characters represent the **group**'s permissions.

- o The final three characters represent **others**' permissions.

4. In our example, –rwxr–xr––, it means the owner has **read**, **write**, and **execute** permissions (rwx), the group has **read** and **execute** permissions (r–x), and others only have **read** permission (r––). This breakdown makes it easy to quickly determine what each user type can do with a file or directory.

5. Permissions are represented by letters: r for **read**, w for **write**, and x for **execute**. But what exactly do these permissions mean in practical terms?

- o **Read** (r) allows a user to view the contents of the file. For a directory, it lets the user list its contents.

- o **Write** (w) allows a user to modify the contents of the file. For a directory, it lets the user create, delete, or rename files within it.

- o **Execute** (x) allows a user to run the file as a program. For a directory, it grants the ability to "enter" the directory and access its contents.

6. These three permissions are combined to form the permission string we saw earlier, and understanding how they work is key to controlling access to your files and directories.

7. Now, let's talk about **changing permissions**. At some point, you'll need to adjust who can access a file or directory, and that's where the chmod command comes in. chmod, short for "change mode," allows you to modify the permissions of a file or directory. You can specify permissions either by using **symbols** or **octal numbers**.
For example, let's say you want to give the owner of a file full access (read, write, and execute), but only allow the group to read and execute, and others to have no access at all. You could use the symbolic method:
bash
Copy

```
chmod u=rwx,g=rx,o= file.txt
```

8.

This command uses u for the user (owner), g for the group, and o for others. The rwx means read, write, and execute; rx means read and execute; and = assigns the exact permissions you specify, removing any previous ones.

9. Alternatively, you can use octal numbers to set permissions more efficiently. In the octal system, each permission is represented by a number: read = 4, write = 2, and execute = 1. The numbers are then added together to form the permission set:

   ○ 7 (4+2+1) means read, write, and execute.

   ○ 5 (4+1) means read and execute.

   ○ 6 (4+2) means read and write.

   ○ 0 means no permission.

10. So, if you want to give the owner full permissions, the group read and execute permissions, and others no permissions, you'd use the following octal command:
bash
Copy

```
chmod 750 file.txt
```

11.

This sets the owner to rwx (7), the group to rx (5), and others to --- (0). Using octal numbers can be quicker and more efficient once you're comfortable with them.

12. You can also **add** or **remove** permissions without modifying the entire permission set. For instance, if you want to add execute permissions to the group, you can use the + symbol:
bash
Copy

```
chmod g+x file.txt
```

13.

This will add the execute permission to the group, leaving all other permissions unchanged. Conversely, if you want to **remove** a permission, you can use the − symbol:
bash
Copy

```
chmod o-x file.txt
```

14.

This will remove execute permission from others.

15. Permissions become even more critical when working with **directories**. In Unix, directories don't just store files—they control access to those files. For example, if you want to allow someone to look at files in a directory but not modify them, you would set the directory's permissions to `r-x` for the group or others. However, without the execute permission (`x`), they won't be able to "enter" the directory and access the files inside it. This highlights the importance of understanding both read and execute permissions for directories. If you're ever unsure, remember: **read** lets you see what's in the directory, and **execute** lets you open it.

16. Permissions also apply to **special files**, like symbolic links and device files. Symbolic links, which you encountered earlier, don't contain data themselves—they point to other files or directories. The permissions on a symlink don't control access to the target file; they only control access to the symlink itself. For example, if you create a symlink pointing to a file you own, others may not be able to modify that file unless they have the proper permissions on the target file. This is why it's important to understand where the symlink points and how permissions apply at both ends.

17. In addition to file and directory permissions, **ownership** is another critical part of Unix's permission system. Every file and directory in Unix has an owner and a group associated with it. By default, when you create a file, you are the owner, and it belongs to your primary group. However, you may need to change ownership from time to time—especially when working with shared resources. The `chown` command allows you to change the owner and group of a file or directory. For example:
bash
Copy

```
chown john:staff file.txt
```

18.

This command changes the owner of `file.txt` to `john` and the group to `staff`. You can also change just the owner or just the group by omitting one of the parameters. This is useful when managing files shared across different users or teams.

19. As you work with Unix systems, you'll find that user and group permissions can get more complex, especially in multi-user environments. This is where the `umask` command comes in. `umask` controls the default permissions for new files and directories. When you create a new file, the system assigns default permissions based on your `umask` setting, and then it subtracts permissions as needed. By adjusting your `umask`, you can control how restrictive or permissive these defaults are. For example, a common `umask` value of `022` will ensure that new files are created with permissions of `644` (read and write for the owner, and read-only for the group and others). Learning how to tweak your `umask` settings is an advanced, but useful, way to automate permission settings for new files.

20. Now that you understand the basics of permissions, let's talk about **security**. One of the most powerful things about Unix is its ability to keep your system secure by restricting access to sensitive files and directories. Permissions allow you to specify exactly who can do what to each file, and when used correctly, they can help protect your system from unauthorized access or accidental modifications. However, with great power comes great responsibility. As you work with permissions, be mindful of how you're granting access. For example, giving the `write` permission to others on a critical configuration file is a bad idea—it can lead to system instability or security risks. Always err on the side of caution, and regularly audit your file permissions to ensure your system remains secure.

21. Permissions also affect how users interact with each other's files. If you're in a multi-user environment, understanding how to set permissions for shared files is essential for collaboration. For example, you might want a file that can be read by everyone but only modified by a specific user. With the right permissions, you can create a file that works just like this. Similarly, when working in a team, using group permissions effectively ensures that everyone who needs access to a particular file or directory has it, while keeping others out.

22. Throughout this chapter, we've explored the world of Unix permissions and how they give you control over your files and system. It may seem like a lot at first, but with practice, it will become second nature. Permissions are the foundation of Unix security and file management, and understanding them is key to working efficiently and safely in the system. As you continue to work with Unix, think of permissions as the keys to your digital kingdom—each file and directory has its own lock, and only the right people can unlock it. Whether you're working alone or collaborating with others, mastering permissions will give you the control you need to manage your system securely and effectively.

23. The next time you encounter a permission issue, you'll know exactly what's going on. You'll understand how to read permission strings, change them with `chmod`, and manage file ownership with `chown`. You'll know how to create secure environments for

your files and directories, ensuring that only the right users have the right level of access. Permissions might seem a little intimidating at first, but now that you've got the knowledge, you can use them to create a secure and efficient system. Remember, in Unix, when it comes to permissions, you're always in control. Just stop and ask yourself, "Who am I?" and "What can I do with this file?" The answer will be at your fingertips.

As you continue to work with permissions, you'll soon realize that understanding them is just the beginning. It's the way you manage and apply them that really makes the difference in keeping your system organized and secure. One of the best practices you'll want to adopt is the principle of least privilege. This principle suggests that you should only grant the minimum permissions necessary for someone (or something) to perform their tasks. For example, if a file only needs to be read by a user, there's no need to give them write permissions. If a process only needs to execute a file, don't grant it the ability to modify it. By limiting permissions, you reduce the potential for accidents or malicious actions. The more you work with permissions, the more you'll understand how granting excessive access can open doors to unwanted risks. Always think before you assign permissions—will this person really need write access, or is read-only enough?

Additionally, Unix gives you the flexibility to fine-tune file access for specific users or groups. One method of doing this is by managing **group permissions**. Groups in Unix are an excellent way to give multiple users access to the same files while maintaining tight control over who can modify those files. For example, if you're working on a collaborative project, you might create a group called `project_team`, and then give that group read and write access to the project's files. You can add as many users as needed to the group, and they will all share the same permissions. This way, you don't have to manage permissions for each user individually, which is especially useful when managing larger teams. By using groups effectively, you'll create a more organized and secure system where access is streamlined and controlled.

One advanced feature that can significantly enhance your control over permissions is the use of **Access Control Lists (ACLs)**. While basic permissions give you a lot of flexibility, ACLs allow you to specify more detailed access rules for files and directories. With ACLs, you can set permissions for individual users or groups beyond just the owner, group, and others. For example, you might have a file that the owner can read and write, the group can only read, and a specific user can read and execute. ACLs provide a finer level of granularity in access control, making them invaluable in complex systems where many users need different levels of access to shared resources. To set ACLs, you'll use the `setfacl` command, and to check ACLs, the `getfacl` command. While ACLs might seem like overkill in simple systems, they're a great tool when you need precise control over file access.

Of course, Unix's permission system isn't without its pitfalls. One common mistake people make is not realizing the implications of file **inheritance**. When you create a new file in a directory, it typically inherits the permissions of the parent directory, but sometimes this inheritance can lead to unexpected results. For example, if you set a directory's permissions to allow everyone to read and write, and then create a new file in that directory, the file might be given write permissions by default. It's important to be mindful of where files are being created and whether their permissions align with what you want. You can use the `umask` command to control the default permissions for new files, but it's still a good idea to check the permissions of any new files or directories, especially when collaborating with others. This is why regularly auditing your system's permissions is key to maintaining a secure environment.

As we wrap up this chapter, let's reflect on how much power you now have over your files and directories. With the knowledge of how to read, modify, and assign permissions, you've unlocked a crucial aspect of Unix. You're not just using a system anymore—you're actively controlling it. Whether you're working on a personal project or managing a multi-user system, understanding permissions ensures that you can keep your data secure while still making it accessible to the right people. Permissions are the gates of your system; they allow you to lock doors and open them only for those who need access. The more you understand how to use them, the more secure and efficient your Unix experience will be.

Don't just stop at mastering the basics. Keep practicing, keep experimenting with different permission sets, and challenge yourself to think about how permissions apply to your specific use case. The more you work with them, the more intuitive they will become. You might even find yourself automating permission changes with scripts or managing access for large teams or systems. The possibilities are endless, and the knowledge of permissions you now possess will be a valuable tool in your Unix toolkit for years to come. In the end, Unix is about empowering you to take control. When you understand the power of permissions, you're not just a user— you're the gatekeeper of your own system.

As a final tip, remember that it's always best to err on the side of caution when it comes to permissions. Over-permissioning can lead to security vulnerabilities, while under-permissioning can prevent legitimate access. Finding the right balance is an ongoing process, and as you gain more experience with Unix, you'll develop a keen sense for which permissions to grant and when. So next time you encounter a file or directory, ask yourself, "Who am I?" and "Who else might need access?" Knowing the answer is the first step toward a safer, more efficient system. And just like that, with a little thought and a lot of practice, you'll be a Unix permission master.

The journey doesn't end here. While permissions are one of the most fundamental parts of Unix, you'll soon learn how they work in conjunction with other features, like user accounts, processes, and networking. Permissions aren't just about locking things down—they're about making sure your system works the way you want it to. From securing sensitive data to collaborating with others, permissions play a huge role in how Unix systems function. As you grow in your knowledge, you'll begin to see how permissions and other system tools fit together to create a powerful, secure, and highly flexible environment. So, keep exploring, keep experimenting, and most importantly—keep asking, "Who am I?" when it comes to managing your files. The more you understand, the more you'll be in control.

Chapter 6: Redirection: Sending Output On A Journey

1. Imagine this: you're standing on a bustling street corner, surrounded by people shouting commands, giving orders, and delivering messages. It's all very chaotic, but there's a trick to it—you can send the messages where you want them to go. In the world of Unix, that street is the terminal, and those messages are the output of your commands. Redirection is like a traffic control system that takes the output of one command and

sends it to a different destination, whether that's a file, another command, or even to nowhere at all. The beauty of redirection is that it gives you complete control over how and where the information flows. Want to capture the output of a command into a file? You can do that. Want to ignore it entirely? That's possible too. In this chapter, you'll learn how to harness the power of redirection to make your Unix experience even more efficient and flexible. Buckle up—it's time to send some output on a journey!

2. Let's start with the basics: how does output work in Unix? Every time you run a command, the system produces some form of output—whether it's displaying the contents of a directory, the results of a search, or an error message. By default, this output appears on your screen (standard output, or `stdout`). However, sometimes the default behavior isn't enough. Maybe you want to save that output for later, or you want to send it to another command for further processing. This is where redirection comes in—it allows you to send that output to a different destination. Instead of displaying it on the screen, you can redirect it to a file, pipe it into another command, or even throw it away entirely. Redirection is one of the most powerful tools in Unix, and once you understand it, you'll wonder how you ever worked without it.

3. The most common form of redirection is sending the output of a command to a file. This is accomplished with the `>` symbol. For example, let's say you want to list the files in a directory and save that list to a file called `file_list.txt`. Instead of having the list displayed on your screen, you can use:
bash
Copy

```
ls > file_list.txt
```

4.

Now, instead of seeing the output on your terminal, it's saved in `file_list.txt`. The next time you open that file, you'll see the list of files as they appeared when you ran the `ls` command. This is incredibly useful when you need to keep a record of something, such as the output of a long-running command or the results of a search. Instead of re-running the command every time, you've got the output safely stored in a file that you can refer to at any time.

5. But what if you want to **append** output to an existing file, rather than overwriting it completely? Maybe you're logging data and don't want to lose what's already been recorded. To do this, you use the `>>` symbol. For instance, let's say you want to append the list of files in a directory to the same `file_list.txt` file you created earlier. Instead of overwriting the file, you'd use:
bash
Copy

```
ls >> file_list.txt
```

6.

Now, the output of this command is added to the end of `file_list.txt`, preserving the contents that were already there. This is perfect for situations like logging where you want to keep a running record of commands without losing previous entries.

7. But redirection isn't just about files—it can also be used to redirect the output of a command to another command. This is called **piping**, and it's one of the most powerful features in Unix. Piping is done with the pipe symbol (|), and it allows you to take the output of one command and send it directly as input to another command. For example, let's say you want to list all the files in a directory but only want to see the ones that end with `.txt`. You could use the `grep` command in combination with `ls` like this:
bash
Copy

```
ls | grep ".txt"
```

8.

In this case, the output of `ls` (the list of files) is piped directly into `grep`, which filters it to only show files that contain `.txt` in their names. This is where the magic of Unix comes into play—by combining commands, you can create powerful workflows that make your tasks much more efficient.

9. But why stop at just piping the output of `ls` into `grep`? You can chain multiple commands together, creating more complex pipelines. For example, imagine you want to count how many `.txt` files are in a directory. You could combine `ls`, `grep`, and `wc` (word count) like this:
bash
Copy

```
ls | grep ".txt" | wc -l
```

10.

Here, `ls` lists all files, `grep` filters out the `.txt` files, and `wc -l` counts how many lines of output are generated, giving you the total number of `.txt` files in the directory. This is just one example of how you can use pipes to create a chain of commands that work together to perform more complex tasks. The possibilities are endless!

11. While we've been focusing on output redirection, it's also important to talk about **error redirection**. Sometimes, commands generate error messages that you don't want to display on your screen, or you might want to redirect them to a file to keep track of issues. Unix treats error messages as a separate stream called **standard error** (or `stderr`), and you can redirect this just like you would standard output. For example, if a command produces an error and you want to save it to a file called `error_log.txt`, you can use:

bash
Copy

```
command 2> error_log.txt
```

12.

The **2>** part tells Unix to redirect **stderr** (stream 2) to `error_log.txt`. If you want to redirect both the output and errors to the same file, you can combine the streams like this:

bash
Copy

```
command > output_log.txt 2>&1
```

13.

This command sends both standard output and standard error to the same file. This is especially useful when you're troubleshooting a command or process, as it keeps all the relevant information in one place.

14. Another handy feature of redirection is the ability to **discard** output entirely. Sometimes, you might run a command that generates a lot of output, but you don't need to see it or save it. Instead of being bombarded by lines and lines of text, you can send the output to **null**. In Unix, `/dev/null` is a special file that discards anything sent to it. To send output to `/dev/null`, you can use:

bash
Copy

```
command > /dev/null
```

15.

This discards the standard output of the command, leaving you with a clean terminal. If you also want to discard error messages, you can redirect both standard output and standard error to /dev/null:

bash

Copy

```
command > /dev/null 2>&1
```

16.

This is a great way to silence commands whose output you don't care about, allowing you to focus on the tasks that matter most.

17. Let's step it up a notch and talk about **input redirection**. While most of the redirection we've discussed so far has been about output, you can also redirect input to a command. For example, instead of typing a list of words directly into a command, you can redirect the contents of a file to the command as input. Let's say you have a file called words.txt containing a list of words, and you want to count how many lines are in the file. Instead of typing the file contents into the wc -l command, you can use input redirection like this:

bash

Copy

```
wc -l < words.txt
```

18.

This sends the contents of words.txt into wc -l as input, and the command will output the number of lines in the file. Input redirection is a great way to feed data into a command without manually entering it each time.

19. Redirection also allows for **combining input and output redirection**. Imagine you're writing a script that processes data from one file and then outputs the results to another file. You can easily combine both input and output redirection. For instance, let's say you

want to process the data in `input.txt`, filter it with `grep`, and then save the results to `output.txt`. You can do this in one step:

```lua
grep "pattern" < input.txt > output.txt
```

In this example, the contents of `input.txt` are fed into `grep` as input, and the output of the `grep` command is saved to `output.txt`. This is a simple example of how input and output redirection can work together to streamline data processing.

11. As you continue to explore redirection, you'll start to realize just how much power it gives you. You're not just limited to capturing and sending output to files or other commands—you can use redirection to create sophisticated workflows, automate tasks, and even manipulate data on the fly. It's the perfect tool for creating custom, one-off tasks or building entire systems of commands that work together to accomplish complex objectives. The key is understanding the many ways redirection can be used to control where data flows and how it gets processed.

12. Let's not forget about the amazing simplicity redirection brings to your workflow. In just a few keystrokes, you can capture output, filter data, discard unnecessary information, or automate repetitive tasks. Redirection turns a series of complex commands into a smooth and seamless experience, freeing you from manual steps and allowing you to focus on more important tasks. Whether you're working with log files, processing large amounts of data, or just cleaning up the output of a command, redirection makes everything easier and more efficient.

13. One of the most fun things about mastering redirection is discovering new ways to make your workflow more efficient. Need to collect the output of multiple commands into one file? Use `>>` to append. Want to see how a program handles errors? Redirect `stderr` to a log file. The more you experiment with redirection, the more ways you'll find to streamline your work. It's like discovering a secret set of tools hidden in plain sight, each one waiting to make your Unix life easier.

14. As you continue to hone your skills with redirection, it will become second nature. You'll be able to chain commands together with pipes, send output to files, redirect errors, and fine-tune your process flows with ease. You'll soon find that redirection isn't just a feature of Unix—it's a core concept that makes working with the command line both powerful and intuitive. And best of all, the more you practice, the more control you'll gain over how data moves through your system.

15. So there you have it—redirection in all its glory. It might seem simple at first, but the possibilities are endless once you begin to experiment with it. Whether you're redirecting output to files, piping it to other commands, or discarding it altogether, redirection is one of the most essential tools in your Unix toolkit. So get out there, start redirecting, and send your data on a journey. The power is in your hands!

16. Now that you understand the basics of redirection, let's explore a few more advanced uses that will take your command line skills to the next level. One powerful feature you might encounter is **here documents**, also known as **heredocs**. A heredoc allows you to redirect multiple lines of input to a command, and it's incredibly useful when you need to provide complex input for commands like `cat`, `echo`, or other programs that process input. Instead of manually typing a list of values or commands, you can create a block of text within your script or command line. Here's how you can use it:

```bash
Copy
cat <<EOF
This is line one
This is line two
And here's line three
EOF
```

This example sends multiple lines of text to `cat`, which will print them to the screen. The EOF marker is just a label, and you can use any word you like to mark the beginning and end of the input block. Heredocs are incredibly handy when you want to include multiple lines of data without creating a separate file, and they're frequently used in scripting.

17. Another cool feature of redirection is the ability to **redirect output to multiple locations** at once. If you want to save output to a file while also displaying it on your screen, you can use the `tee` command. `tee` is a command that reads from standard input and writes to both standard output (your terminal screen) and a file. For example, if you want to see the output of a command while saving it to a file, you could do this:

```bash
Copy
ls | tee file_list.txt
```

This will list the files in the current directory, display them on the screen, and save the list to `file_list.txt` at the same time. `tee` is particularly useful for logging purposes—imagine running a long script or process, and you want to save its output while still seeing it as it happens. With `tee`, you can do both without any extra effort. If you need to append output to a file rather than overwrite it, simply use the `-a` flag, like so:

```bash
Copy
ls | tee -a file_list.txt
```

This appends the output to `file_list.txt` without clearing the previous content, giving you a running log of all the data.

18. Sometimes, you'll want to **combine multiple streams** of output in a more complex way. For example, let's say you have both standard output and error output and you want to combine them in a single file, but you want to maintain control over how they are

handled. You can redirect both output streams and merge them using a technique called **file descriptor manipulation**. Here's how you do it:

```bash
Copy
command > output.txt 2>&1
```

The `> output.txt` part redirects the standard output to a file. The `2>&1` part redirects **stderr** (stream 2) to the same place as **stdout** (stream 1). This way, both error messages and regular output go into `output.txt`. This is useful when you need to capture everything happening during a process in a single file, especially when troubleshooting or logging.

19. As you continue to use redirection, one thing you'll start to notice is how it can help you **automate tasks**. Instead of interacting with a program in real-time, you can redirect input and output to files, making it possible to schedule and automate processes with tools like `cron`. Imagine you're running a backup process that generates logs—rather than sitting there to watch it happen, you can set it to run automatically and redirect the output to a log file. You can check the log at your convenience to see if the process completed successfully. Redirection allows you to create hands-off workflows, so you don't need to monitor everything manually.

20. Another great feature to remember when using redirection is how it simplifies the **debugging process**. When you're working with complex scripts or systems that produce a lot of output, having the ability to redirect and filter this output to different files or processes can help you quickly identify issues. For example, if a program is producing both normal output and error messages, you can separate them by redirecting each to different files:

```bash
Copy
command > output.txt 2> error_log.txt
```

By saving errors and regular output in separate files, you can review the logs later to see where things went wrong. This separation can save you a lot of time when troubleshooting, especially if you're dealing with long-running processes or programs that produce lots of data.

21. Redirection also plays a huge role in **data processing**. Often, you'll find yourself working with large data files, whether they're logs, text files, or system reports. Instead of manually editing or sorting through them, you can use redirection in combination with other commands like `grep`, `awk`, or `sed` to process and analyze the data in real-time. For example, if you have a huge log file and you want to extract only certain entries, you can use:

```bash
Copy
cat huge_log.txt | grep "ERROR" > error_log.txt
```

This command will take the contents of `huge_log.txt`, pipe them through `grep` to find only the lines that contain "ERROR," and then redirect that filtered output to `error_log.txt`. This makes data extraction and processing much easier and more efficient.

22. As you become more experienced with redirection, you'll begin to recognize how it opens up a world of possibilities for improving your workflow. Redirection isn't just about saving output to a file—it's about controlling the flow of information within your system. It's about filtering, automating, and optimizing how data is processed and stored. Whether you're running scripts, managing logs, or simply organizing files, redirection gives you the tools to do it all. It's like having a personal assistant who can automatically sort and organize data exactly the way you want it.

23. One of the most satisfying things about mastering redirection is how it simplifies tasks that once felt tedious or repetitive. By redirecting output to files, you can easily keep records of your actions. By piping output between commands, you can create complex workflows without having to manually intervene. And by discarding unnecessary output or errors, you can keep your terminal clean and focused on what really matters. As you continue to work with Unix, you'll realize just how much time redirection saves you, allowing you to focus on the more important aspects of your work.

24. So far, we've only scratched the surface of what redirection can do. The more you explore, the more you'll find ways to integrate redirection into your day-to-day tasks. The beauty of redirection is that it's a tool that can adapt to any workflow, from the simplest tasks to the most complex operations. As you dive deeper into Unix, you'll uncover even more advanced techniques for manipulating and controlling data. Redirection is one of the core concepts that makes Unix so powerful, and the more you use it, the more natural it will feel.

25. To wrap up this chapter, remember that redirection is more than just a simple tool—it's the key to unlocking a world of efficiency and control in your Unix experience. By redirecting output and input, chaining commands together, and automating tasks, you'll make your work faster and more powerful. Whether you're logging system data, processing files, or troubleshooting errors, redirection will be there to help. So, the next time you run a command, take a moment to think about where that output should go—because in the world of Unix, it's not just about what you do, but how you send it on its journey. Happy redirecting!

Chapter 7: More Than a File: Directories, Links, and Shortcuts

1. By now, you're familiar with files in Unix—those containers for data that we work with daily. But files are only part of the story. In fact, the Unix file system isn't just a collection of files; it's a structured, hierarchical system where files and directories interact with each other in ways that give Unix its power and flexibility. Think of a directory as a filing cabinet, and inside that filing cabinet are files and even other directories. Just like a well-organized office with labeled folders and subfolders, the directory structure in Unix keeps everything neat and easy to find. But there's more than just organization going on

here. Directories serve as the framework for the entire system, and without them, Unix would be nothing more than a pile of disorganized files. In this chapter, we're going to explore the world of directories, how they're created, navigated, and used, as well as some powerful tools like symbolic links and shortcuts that will make your Unix life even more efficient.

2. Let's start with the basics of **directories**. In Unix, a directory is essentially a container for files and other directories. The file system is structured in a hierarchical way, starting from the **root directory** (`/`) and branching out into subdirectories. This structure is like a tree, where the root is the trunk and directories are branches, some of which may have their own sub-branches (subdirectories). For example, you might have a directory called `/home` for user files, and inside that, you'll find subdirectories for each user, like `/home/john` or `/home/alice`. Inside each of these user directories, there may be more directories—like `Documents`, `Downloads`, or `Pictures`. As you explore the system, you'll notice that directories help organize files and make the whole structure more manageable. Understanding how to navigate and work with these directories is essential to becoming proficient in Unix.

3. One of the most important concepts in navigating directories is understanding **absolute** vs. **relative** paths. An absolute path starts from the root directory and specifies the complete path to a file or directory. For example, `/home/john/Documents` is an absolute path because it starts from the root directory (`/`) and leads directly to the `Documents` directory within the `john` user's home directory. In contrast, a **relative path** specifies the location of a file or directory relative to your current directory. For example, if you are currently in `/home/john` and want to move into the `Documents` folder, you can simply type `cd Documents` because it's relative to your current location. Knowing when to use absolute vs. relative paths will save you time and make navigation more efficient, especially as you work deeper into the Unix file system.

4. Navigating directories is easy once you've learned the `cd` command, but what if you want to see the contents of a directory? That's where the `ls` command comes in. The `ls` command lists all files and subdirectories in the current directory. For example, running `ls` inside `/home/john` will show you all the files and directories in the `john` directory. But `ls` has many options that can make your life even easier. You can use `ls -l` for a more detailed listing, which shows file permissions, ownership, size, and modification time. Or, if you want to include hidden files (those starting with a dot), you can use `ls -a`. The more familiar you become with `ls`, the more you'll appreciate how it helps you explore the contents of directories quickly and efficiently.

5. Another useful tool for navigating directories is the **tab completion** feature. This feature automatically completes file and directory names for you as you type, saving you time and preventing errors. For example, if you start typing `cd /home/joh`, you can press the `Tab` key, and the terminal will automatically complete the path to `/home/john`. If

there are multiple matches, pressing `Tab` twice will show you a list of possible completions. Tab completion is a huge time-saver, especially when you're working with long or complex directory names. It's one of those little features that quickly becomes indispensable once you start using it regularly.

6. As you get more familiar with directories, you'll probably want to create, move, or delete them. To create a new directory, use the `mkdir` command followed by the name of the directory you want to create. For example, `mkdir Projects` creates a new directory called `Projects` in your current location. Want to create a directory in a different location? Simply provide the full path, like `mkdir /home/john/Projects`. To delete an empty directory, use `rmdir`. However, if the directory contains files or other directories, you'll need to use `rm -r`, which recursively deletes the contents along with the directory itself. Be careful with this command—once a directory is deleted, it's gone for good.

7. But what if you need to **link** to a directory or file without actually duplicating it? Unix offers two powerful tools for this: **symbolic links** and **hard links**. A **symbolic link**, or **symlink**, is like a shortcut that points to another file or directory. When you access a symlink, the system follows the link to the actual file or directory. To create a symlink, use the `ln -s` command. For example:
    bash
    Copy

    ```
    ln -s /home/john/Documents /home/john/Projects/
    Documents_Link
    ```

8.

    This creates a symlink called `Documents_Link` in the `Projects` directory that points to the original `Documents` directory. When you navigate to `Documents_Link`, it will behave just like the original `Documents` directory. Symlinks are incredibly useful for creating shortcuts, organizing your files, and linking to shared resources without duplicating data.

9. On the other hand, a **hard link** is a direct reference to a file on the file system. Unlike symlinks, which point to files or directories, hard links are essentially additional names for the same file. When you create a hard link, the system creates a second entry for the file, but both links point to the same data on the disk. If you modify one link, the changes are reflected in the other link as well. To create a hard link, you can use the `ln` command without the `-s` option:
    bash
    Copy

```
ln /home/john/file.txt /home/john/Projects/
file_link.txt
```

10.

This creates a hard link called `file_link.txt` that points directly to `file.txt`. Hard links are useful when you want multiple references to the same file, but be cautious: if you delete the original file, the data remains accessible through the hard link. It's also important to note that hard links cannot be created for directories (except for the special `.` and `..` links) and cannot span across different file systems.

11. Now that you've learned about links, let's talk about the concept of **shortcuts**. In Unix, shortcuts are often created using symbolic links, as we've discussed, but there are other ways to create quick access points to frequently used files or directories. One of the simplest methods is by using **aliases**. An alias is a shortcut to a command or series of commands, making it easier to run complex or frequently used commands. For example, you can create an alias to list files in a directory in long format with `ls -l` by typing:

bash
Copy

```
alias ll="ls -l"
```

12.

Now, every time you type `ll`, it's as if you typed `ls -l`. Aliases can save you time and effort, especially when you work with long or complicated commands. To make your aliases permanent, you can add them to your `.bashrc` file in your home directory. This way, they will be available every time you open a terminal.

13. Another useful shortcut comes in the form of **environment variables**. These variables store system-wide or user-specific values that you can reference in your commands. For example, `$HOME` is an environment variable that stores the path to your home directory. Instead of typing `/home/john` every time you want to reference your home directory, you can use `$HOME`, which makes your commands more flexible. To see all your environment variables, simply type `printenv` or `env`. You can also create your own custom environment variables by adding them to your `.bashrc` file. These custom variables can act as shortcuts for paths, frequently used commands, or any other values you need to store.

14. By now, you've learned how to navigate directories, create links and shortcuts, and organize your files with ease. Directories are the foundation of the Unix file system, and understanding how to use them effectively will help you manage your files more efficiently. Whether you're working on personal projects, managing a team, or organizing system files, directories and links provide the structure and flexibility needed to keep everything in order. But even more than that, they give you the freedom to customize your workflow, create shortcuts, and automate repetitive tasks.

15. As you continue to work with directories, links, and shortcuts, don't forget about **directory permissions**. Just like files, directories have their own permissions, and understanding how to manage those permissions is essential to keeping your system secure. For example, you might want to restrict access to certain directories or allow multiple users to collaborate in shared directories. You can use the same `chmod` command to change directory permissions and the `chown` command to modify ownership, ensuring that only the right people have access to the right directories.

16. The more you experiment with directories and links, the more you'll see how powerful Unix can be when it comes to organizing, navigating, and interacting with your files. Directories help you keep things structured, symlinks and hard links provide shortcuts, and environment variables and aliases allow you to streamline your workflow. By mastering these tools, you'll unlock a level of efficiency and organization that would be impossible with just a simple file manager.

17. So, take a moment to explore your system and see how directories and links work for you. Create new directories, experiment with symlinks, and organize your files in ways that suit your workflow. With these tools at your disposal, you'll be able to navigate the file system like a pro, making your Unix experience smoother, faster, and more organized. The world of directories, links, and shortcuts is waiting for you—so go ahead, dive in, and make it your own!

18. As you explore more advanced uses of directories and links, you'll start to realize how indispensable these tools are when working in complex environments. For instance, when you're dealing with multiple projects or large systems, symlinks can simplify your workflow by allowing you to access commonly used files or directories from different locations without duplicating them. Say, for example, you're working on two different projects that share a common resources directory. Instead of copying the resources into each project, you can create symlinks pointing to the same resources directory in both project directories. This not only saves disk space but also ensures that any updates to the resource directory are reflected across all linked projects.

19. Another benefit of symlinks is that they make it much easier to manage shared files across different systems. Let's say you're working in a multi-machine environment, and certain files need to be accessed by multiple users across different systems. Rather than copying those files to each machine, you can use symlinks that point to a shared network drive or a remote location. The best part is that the symlink will remain the same no matter how the file is accessed, whether from a local or remote system. This level of

flexibility can save you considerable time when working with distributed systems, and it's a great example of how Unix's approach to file management and links can simplify complex tasks.

20. Symlinks also shine in situations where you need to maintain compatibility between different software versions. For example, let's say a program depends on a specific version of a library, but you want to use a newer version. Instead of manually updating every reference to the old library in the program, you can create a symlink that points to the new version. The program will continue to reference the symlink, which can be updated to point to the correct version of the library without needing to change the program's configuration or code. This flexibility makes Unix an ideal environment for handling the complexities of software dependencies.

21. But symlinks aren't without their challenges. One potential pitfall is broken symlinks. If the target of a symlink is moved or deleted, the symlink will no longer work, and you'll end up with a "dangling" symlink that points to nowhere. To avoid this, it's good practice to periodically check for broken symlinks, especially in large systems or projects where files might be frequently moved or deleted. To identify broken symlinks, you can use the `find` command with the `-xtype` option, like so:

bash
Copy
```
find /path/to/directory -xtype l
```
This will list any symlinks that are pointing to nonexistent files. Regularly checking your symlinks and updating them when necessary will help ensure that your file system remains clean and efficient.

22. Another important concept to understand is the difference between **relative symlinks** and **absolute symlinks**. An **absolute symlink** contains the full path to the target file or directory, starting from the root directory. For example:

bash
Copy
```
ln -s /home/john/Documents/project /home/john/Projects/
ProjectLink
```
This symlink always points to `/home/john/Documents/project`, regardless of where it is accessed from. In contrast, a **relative symlink** contains the path to the target file or directory relative to the symlink's location. For example:

bash
Copy
```
ln -s ../Documents/project ./ProjectLink
```
This relative symlink works as long as the symlink is in the same location relative to the target. If you move the symlink or the target, you may break the relative link, so it's important to understand the implications of using relative versus absolute symlinks, especially in larger systems where files and directories may be moved around.

23. As you continue to experiment with symlinks, it's worth noting that they can also be used in more advanced file system management tasks. For example, when managing a server, you might need to set up symlinks to make configuration files easier to manage or to provide access to commonly used files in multiple locations. One common use case is managing log files: sysadmins often create symlinks to ensure that log files are rotated correctly and that old log files can be easily accessed and managed without having to manually track down different file versions. By understanding symlinks, you'll gain a powerful tool for managing your system and its resources more efficiently.

24. As we shift our focus back to directories, it's essential to remember that directories are more than just places to store files. Directories themselves have important roles in how Unix organizes and secures the system. For example, directories can be used to organize your system by purpose or function—system files might be stored in `/etc`, application binaries might reside in `/usr/bin`, and user data is often stored in `/home`. Understanding this structure will help you quickly find the files or directories you need, and it will give you the knowledge you need to maintain a well-organized system.

25. Another key concept is the idea of **directory permissions**. Just as files have permissions controlling who can read, write, or execute them, directories have their own set of permissions that determine who can access, modify, or create files within them. For example, if you have a directory where only you should be able to add or remove files, you would set the directory's permissions accordingly, ensuring that others can't make changes. Similarly, if you're working on a collaborative project, you might want to grant read and write access to a directory for a group of users while restricting access for others. Directory permissions are crucial for maintaining a secure and organized system, and understanding how to manage them is essential for every Unix user.

26. Moving beyond basic directories and symlinks, Unix offers a unique method of organizing files called the **filesystem hierarchy**. In this structure, files and directories are organized according to specific conventions, which helps ensure that system files, user files, and configuration files are easily identifiable and accessible. For example, system-wide configuration files are typically stored in `/etc`, whereas user-specific configuration files are stored in `~/.config`. By adhering to these conventions, Unix makes it easier to find and manage files across different systems, ensuring that your system remains consistent and portable. This hierarchical structure also makes it easier to back up or migrate files—if you know where everything belongs, you can quickly copy only the necessary files, without worrying about accidentally leaving something important behind.

27. As you delve deeper into the Unix file system, you'll begin to appreciate the power and flexibility that directories, links, and shortcuts provide. Whether you're managing personal projects, maintaining a server, or building a custom environment, understanding how to create and navigate directories, set up symlinks, and use shortcuts will make your life significantly easier. These tools help you organize your files, manage your resources efficiently, and navigate your system with precision. By mastering these techniques, you're taking control of your file system and unlocking the full potential of Unix.

28. The beauty of directories, links, and shortcuts in Unix is that they allow you to work in a way that's customized to your needs. Whether you prefer working with absolute paths for consistency or relative paths for portability, whether you rely on symlinks to streamline your workflow or use aliases to create shortcuts for long commands, the flexibility these tools offer will make you more productive and efficient. As you continue to explore the world of Unix, keep these tools in mind—because with the right organization and shortcuts, you'll find that navigating and managing your system becomes second nature. Go ahead, experiment with directories, links, and shortcuts, and make your Unix environment work for you. The possibilities are endless!

Chapter 8: Creating Files: More Than Just Copy-Pasting

1. So far, you've learned a lot about navigating the Unix file system, managing permissions, and working with directories. But now it's time to talk about creating files—because in the world of Unix, creating files is not just about copy-pasting or dragging and dropping. It's about having full control over your files and knowing the most efficient ways to create, edit, and manage them. Whether you're working with simple text files, complex scripts, or configuration files, knowing how to create files in Unix opens up a whole new level of flexibility and control. By the end of this chapter, you'll not only be able to create files, but you'll also understand how to manipulate them, organize them, and use them in powerful ways. Let's get started!

2. The simplest way to create a file in Unix is using the `touch` command. At first glance, `touch` might seem like an odd name for a file-creation command, but it's actually one of the most useful tools for quickly creating empty files. When you run `touch filename`, it creates an empty file called `filename` in your current directory. For example, typing `touch example.txt` will create an empty text file named `example.txt`. But here's the kicker: `touch` isn't just for creating new files—it's also useful for updating the timestamps of existing files. If you want to refresh the modification time of a file without altering its contents, `touch` comes in handy. So, it's a double-duty tool that's perfect for quickly getting a new file or updating an old one.

3. While `touch` creates an empty file, in many cases, you'll want to add content to your file right away. In Unix, you have several options for adding content to files without needing to open a complex text editor. One way to add content is by using the `echo` command. As you know from previous chapters, `echo` is great for printing text to the terminal, but you can also use it to add text directly to a file. For example, let's say you want to create a new file called `notes.txt` and immediately add a line of text to it. You could do this:

```bash
Copy
```

```
echo "This is my first note" > notes.txt
```

4.

This command writes the text "This is my first note" to the file `notes.txt`. If the file doesn't exist, `echo` creates it. If the file already exists, the `>` symbol overwrites it with the new content. If you want to append to the file instead of overwriting it, simply use `>>`:

```bash
Copy
```

```
echo "Adding a second note" >> notes.txt
```

5.

This appends the new text to the end of the file. Using `echo` for creating and managing simple files is a quick and easy way to get started.

6. Of course, when you're working with larger files or more complex content, you'll need a real text editor. Fortunately, Unix has several excellent editors, and while there are many options to choose from, two of the most popular are `nano` and `vim`. Both of these editors allow you to create, modify, and save files, but they operate very differently.

7. **Nano** is a beginner-friendly, easy-to-use text editor that operates entirely in the terminal. To create or edit a file with `nano`, simply type `nano filename`. For example, if you want to create a file called `todo.txt`, you'd type:

```bash
Copy
```

```
nano todo.txt
```

8.

This opens `nano` and allows you to start typing your content directly into the file. Once you're done, you can save your file by pressing `Ctrl + O`, then exit the editor by pressing `Ctrl + X`. Nano provides helpful keyboard shortcuts at the bottom of the screen, making it easy for beginners to quickly learn the ropes. If you're creating a simple text file or making quick edits, `nano` is a great choice.

9. On the other hand, **Vim** is a more advanced text editor that offers a lot of features for those willing to learn its powerful set of commands. While it has a steeper learning curve, `vim` is beloved by many Unix power users for its efficiency and speed. To start a file

with `vim`, type:

bash

```
vim example.txt
```

10.

This opens the file in `vim`, and you can start typing your content. However, `vim` operates in different modes—**insert mode** for typing and **command mode** for editing commands. You can press `i` to enter insert mode, type your content, and then press `Esc` to return to command mode. When you're done, you can save your file by typing `:w` and quit by typing `:q`. To save and quit in one step, type `:wq`. While `vim` might be a bit intimidating at first, it's an incredibly powerful tool once you get the hang of it, and it's worth investing time to learn.

11. While text editors like `nano` and `vim` are excellent for creating and modifying text files, sometimes you'll want to create files without having to manually type them out. For instance, if you need to generate a configuration file or some data automatically, you can use **redirection** or **command output** to create files. For example, if you want to generate a list of all files in a directory and save it to a file, you can use the `ls` command in combination with redirection:

bash

```
ls > file_list.txt
```

12.

This command runs `ls`, which lists all files in the current directory, and redirects the output to a file called `file_list.txt`. This way, you can generate files dynamically based on the output of commands, which is extremely useful for system administration or automating tasks.

13. If you need to **copy** the contents of one file to another, Unix provides an efficient tool for that: the `cp` command. The `cp` command allows you to copy a file from one location to another. For example, if you want to copy `notes.txt` to `backup_notes.txt`, you can run:

bash

```
cp notes.txt backup_notes.txt
```

14.

This copies the content of `notes.txt` into `backup_notes.txt`. If the destination file already exists, it will be overwritten unless you use the `-i` option to prompt for confirmation before overwriting. The `cp` command can also be used to copy entire directories using the `-r` option, which is useful when you need to back up or duplicate multiple files at once.

15. While copying files is useful, you may sometimes need to **move** or **rename** files. For this, the `mv` command is your go-to tool. The `mv` command allows you to move files between directories, or rename them if needed. For example, to move `notes.txt` from your current directory to the `Documents` directory, you can run:
bash
Copy

```
mv notes.txt ~/Documents
```

16.

This moves the file into the `Documents` folder. If you want to rename a file, simply provide the new name as the destination:
bash
Copy

```
mv old_name.txt new_name.txt
```

17.

The `mv` command can be used for both file movement and renaming, which makes it one of the most versatile commands in your Unix toolbox.

18. If you need to **delete** a file, you can use the `rm` (remove) command. For example, to delete a file called `oldfile.txt`, you can run:
bash
Copy

```
rm oldfile.txt
```

19.

Be cautious with `rm`, though, as files deleted with this command are permanently removed—they don't go to the trash. If you want to be extra cautious, you can use the `-i` option to prompt for confirmation before deleting each file:

bash
Copy

```
rm -i oldfile.txt
```

20.

And if you're dealing with a directory, you'll need to use the `-r` (recursive) option to delete the directory and all its contents:

bash
Copy

```
rm -r directory_name
```

21.

22. When creating files, you may encounter cases where you need to define their **permissions** right away. The `chmod` command lets you control access to the files you create. For example, if you've just created a script file and want to make it executable, you would use:

bash
Copy

```
chmod +x script.sh
```

23.

This command adds execute permissions for the file, allowing you (and others, depending on the permissions) to run the script as a program. Permissions can be set when creating files, or modified later, to control who can read, write, or execute them. Understanding how to use `chmod` is crucial for managing access to your files and keeping your system secure.

24. The **ownership** of files is another important concept to consider when creating files. When you create a file, you are automatically assigned as the owner of that file. However, if you need to change the ownership of a file (for example, if you're collaborating on a project with other users), you can use the `chown` command:

bash
Copy

```
chown newuser:newgroup filename.txt
```

25.

This changes the owner of the file to `newuser` and the group to `newgroup`. Changing file ownership allows you to control who can modify or manage files, and it's especially useful when working in a multi-user environment.

26. Finally, creating files isn't just about making new text documents or code. As you explore Unix more, you'll likely need to interact with **binary files**, such as compiled programs, system files, and even images or media files. While text files are easy to create and edit directly in the terminal, working with binary files requires specialized tools and knowledge. For now, focus on mastering the basic techniques of creating and managing text files, and as you get more comfortable with Unix, you'll naturally expand your skillset to handle more complex file types.

27. To wrap up this chapter, creating files in Unix is much more than just copy-pasting. It's about understanding how to use the right tools to create, edit, manage, and control your files effectively. Whether you're using `touch` for empty files, `echo` for quick content, or advanced text editors like `nano` and `vim`, you now have the knowledge to create and manipulate files like a Unix pro. Combine this with the ability to copy, move, delete, and control permissions, and you'll have full control over your file system. Keep practicing these commands, and soon you'll be creating files that work for you, not the other way around.

28. As you continue to explore file creation in Unix, it's important to understand how to handle **file content efficiently**. Beyond just creating files and adding text, you'll often need to edit files or work with large amounts of data. While editors like `nano` and `vim` are great for interactive editing, Unix also provides powerful command-line tools to manipulate file content without opening a text editor.

29. One of the most commonly used tools for modifying file content is **sed** (stream editor). `sed` allows you to perform text transformations on files or streams of data. For example, if you have a file and you want to replace every instance of "apple" with "orange," you can use `sed` to do this with a single command:

bash
Copy

```
sed -i 's/apple/orange/g' file.txt
```

30.

The `-i` option tells `sed` to modify the file directly. The `s/apple/orange/g` part specifies that "apple" should be replaced with "orange" globally (i.e., every instance in the file). `sed` is incredibly powerful for automating text manipulations, and it's a great tool for batch processing files without needing to open them in a text editor.

31. Another useful tool for file content manipulation is **awk**. `awk` is a versatile programming language designed for pattern scanning and processing. It is often used for working with column-based data, such as CSV files or log files. For example, if you have a file with data separated by spaces or tabs, and you want to print the first column, you can use `awk` like this:

bash
Copy

```
awk '{print $1}' file.txt
```

32.

This command will print the first column of data in `file.txt`. `awk` can do much more, from performing arithmetic on file contents to filtering lines based on conditions. It's a must-know tool for anyone working with data files in Unix.

33. For more advanced file editing, **vi** (or **vim**, the improved version of `vi`) is one of the most widely used editors. While `nano` is friendly for beginners, `vim` is an advanced editor that can be fully controlled with the keyboard, making it faster and more efficient for many tasks. `vim` allows you to manipulate files with complex commands and even automate repetitive editing tasks with its built-in scripting capabilities. Learning `vim` can significantly speed up your workflow, especially when dealing with large files or performing advanced text processing. Don't be intimidated by its initial complexity; once

you become familiar with the key commands, `vim` becomes a powerful tool for editing and creating files directly from the terminal.

34. When you're working with files that need to be **backed up** or **duplicated**, the `cp` command is your go-to tool for making copies. You can copy a single file, or you can use `cp -r` to recursively copy entire directories. If you want to copy multiple files at once, you can specify each file in the command:

```bash
Copy


cp file1.txt file2.txt file3.txt /path/to/destination/
```

35.

This command copies `file1.txt`, `file2.txt`, and `file3.txt` into the destination directory. You can also use the `-i` option to make `cp` ask for confirmation before overwriting any existing files in the destination. This is useful for preventing accidental data loss when working with important files.

36. One of the key aspects of working with files is knowing how to **organize** them. As you work with more files, it's easy for things to get cluttered. That's where directories and proper naming conventions come into play. Group related files into directories, and use clear and descriptive names for your files. By keeping your system organized, you can avoid wasting time searching for files, and you'll reduce the chances of accidentally overwriting or losing important data. As you get more experienced with Unix, you'll develop your own methods for structuring files and directories in a way that suits your workflow.

37. In addition to organizing files, **permissions** are critical when creating and managing files. Permissions determine who can read, write, and execute files. When you create a new file, you're assigned ownership of that file by default, but you may need to change the file's permissions or ownership when working in a multi-user environment. The `chmod` and `chown` commands allow you to modify permissions and ownership, ensuring that only authorized users have access to sensitive files. As you continue to work with files, make sure you're familiar with how permissions work and how to use them to secure your files and directories.

38. As you start working with more complex files, such as configuration files or scripts, you may find it helpful to **version control** your files. Version control systems, such as Git, allow you to keep track of changes to files over time, so you can easily revert to previous versions if something goes wrong. Using version control is especially important when you're working on collaborative projects, as it lets you track who made what changes and

when. It's a good habit to start versioning your files early, especially when you're working on scripts, configuration files, or any project that requires ongoing development.

39. When creating files, it's also important to understand **file encodings** and **line endings**. Different operating systems may use different formats for encoding text or indicating the end of a line. For instance, Windows uses `CRLF` (Carriage Return and Line Feed) for line endings, while Unix and Linux use just `LF` (Line Feed). These differences can cause issues when transferring files between systems. Tools like `dos2unix` and `unix2dos` can convert between these formats, ensuring that your files are compatible across different environments. Understanding these nuances will help you avoid unexpected formatting issues when working with text files.

40. At this point, you've learned how to create files in a variety of ways, from simple empty files with `touch` to adding content using `echo` or creating complex files with text editors like `nano` and `vim`. You've also learned how to manage file content with powerful tools like `sed` and `awk`, and how to copy, move, and organize files using Unix's intuitive command-line tools. With these skills, you now have the ability to manage files with greater flexibility and efficiency than ever before.

41. Remember, creating files in Unix is more than just a process—it's about controlling how your data is structured, accessed, and manipulated. The tools and techniques you've learned in this chapter are just the beginning. As you continue to grow as a Unix user, you'll discover even more ways to work with files, automate tasks, and integrate your workflow with other systems. So, whether you're creating simple text files, configuring your system, or developing complex scripts, always remember that Unix gives you the power to make your files work for you—your way.

Chapter 9: Understanding Processes: The Magic Behind the Scenes

1. Every time you run a command in Unix, whether it's listing files, editing text, or running a script, you're triggering a **process**. But what exactly is a process, and why does it matter? At its core, a process is simply an instance of a running program. It's a program that has been loaded into memory, executed by the system, and is actively doing its job. Just like a busy worker in an office, processes are constantly running in the background, performing tasks that allow your system to function. Understanding processes is key to becoming a proficient Unix user because it gives you insight into how your system works, how to manage resources efficiently, and how to troubleshoot problems. In this chapter, we'll pull back the curtain on processes and uncover the magic behind the scenes.

2. Let's start with the basics: what happens when you execute a command? When you type a command and hit `Enter`, the system creates a **process** to carry out that command. This process is assigned a unique identifier called a **PID** (Process ID), which allows the system to track and manage it. The process will then execute the program and produce the result you expect—whether it's displaying output on the screen, modifying a file, or

performing some other task. But processes don't live forever. Once the task is completed, the process finishes and terminates, freeing up the system resources it was using. The life cycle of a process might seem simple, but in a multi-user, multi-tasking system like Unix, things get more complex quickly.

3.   Unix is a multitasking system, meaning it can run multiple processes simultaneously. The operating system's **kernel** is in charge of managing all of these processes, ensuring that each one gets its fair share of CPU time, memory, and other resources. It uses a technique called **scheduling** to decide which process should run next. The kernel switches between processes very quickly, often so fast that it seems like everything is running at the same time. This is why Unix is so efficient—it can juggle many tasks at once, allowing you to run programs, perform background tasks, and interact with the system all simultaneously. In fact, when you're running a command in the terminal, that command is just one of many processes in the system.

4.   So, how do you view and manage the processes running on your system? The `ps` command is your window into the world of processes. By default, `ps` shows you a snapshot of the processes running in your current terminal session. For example, if you type:
bash
Copy

```
ps
```

5.

You'll see a list of processes associated with your terminal session. Each entry will include the process ID (PID), the terminal from which the process was started, the running time, and the command that started the process. If you want to see a more detailed list of all running processes on the system, you can use the `-e` flag:
bash
Copy

```
ps -e
```

6.

This will show all processes, regardless of which terminal they belong to. Want to see even more detailed information? Try `ps -aux`, which provides additional details such as memory and CPU usage, the user who owns each process, and more. `ps` is an invaluable command for anyone looking to monitor and manage processes.

7. While `ps` is great for a snapshot of processes, sometimes you'll need to see a real-time view of what's happening on your system. For that, the `top` command is your friend. When you run `top`, it continuously updates the list of running processes, showing their CPU and memory usage, their PID, and other vital stats. It's an excellent tool for monitoring system performance and identifying any processes that are hogging resources. For example, if your system is running slow and you want to figure out which process is consuming all the CPU, `top` will give you the real-time data you need to track it down. You can even interact with `top` while it's running—press `q` to quit, or use other keys to sort and filter processes.

8. Once you know which processes are running, it's important to understand how to **manage** them. If a process is misbehaving or taking up too much CPU time, you might want to stop it. The `kill` command allows you to terminate processes by sending them a signal. To kill a process, you can use the following command:
bash
Copy

```
kill PID
```

9.

Where `PID` is the process ID of the process you want to stop. For example, if a process with the ID 1234 is causing trouble, you can type `kill 1234` to terminate it. By default, `kill` sends the `SIGTERM` signal, which gracefully asks the process to terminate. However, if the process is stubborn and refuses to die, you can force it to quit with the `-9` option:
bash
Copy

```
kill -9 PID
```

10.

This sends the `SIGKILL` signal, which immediately terminates the process without giving it a chance to clean up. Be careful with `kill -9`, as it can cause data loss if the process is in the middle of writing to a file or performing other important tasks.

11. Processes in Unix are also organized into a hierarchical structure. Every process, except the very first one (the **init** process), is created by another process. The process that starts another process is called its **parent process**, and the created process is called its **child process**. This hierarchy is important because it helps the system manage resources and control the flow of execution. You can view a process's parent ID (PPID) with the `ps` command by adding the `--ppid` option. For example:

bash
Copy

```
ps --ppid 1
```

12.

This command shows you all processes that are children of the process with the PID of 1, which is typically the `init` process (the root of the process tree). Understanding this hierarchy can help you diagnose issues with process management, especially when processes are becoming orphaned or not terminating correctly.

13. In some cases, you might want to run a process in the **background** so that it doesn't block your terminal session. For example, if you're running a long command, you can add an ampersand (`&`) at the end of the command to run it in the background:

bash
Copy

```
long-running-command &
```

14.

This allows you to continue working in the terminal while the command runs in the background. If you want to view all background jobs, you can use the `jobs` command. To bring a background process to the foreground, you can use the `fg` command followed by the job number:

bash
Copy

```
fg %1
```

15.

This brings job 1 (from the list of background jobs) back to the foreground, where it will run interactively.

16. If you want to run a process in the background even after you log out, you can use the **nohup** command. This stands for "no hangup," and it prevents a process from being terminated when you close the terminal. For example:

bash
Copy

```
nohup long-running-command &
```

17.

This will allow the process to continue running after you log out or close the terminal, and the output will be written to a file called `nohup.out` by default. This is especially useful for long-running tasks or server-side processes that need to continue after the user session ends.

18. **Process scheduling** is another important concept when working with processes. In a multitasking operating system like Unix, processes are constantly being switched in and out of the CPU. This is managed by the kernel's scheduler. While most processes are scheduled automatically, you can adjust the priority of processes using the `nice` and `renice` commands. The `nice` command allows you to start a process with a specific priority level. For example, to start a process with a lower priority, you can use:

bash
Copy

```
nice -n 10 command
```

19.

The `-n` option specifies the priority level, with higher numbers indicating lower priority. If you want to change the priority of a running process, you can use `renice`:

bash
Copy

```
renice -n 5 -p PID
```

20.

This changes the priority of the process with the given `PID` to a higher value, making it less CPU-intensive.

21. Processes are an essential part of any operating system, but managing them efficiently requires an understanding of how they work. By learning to use commands like `ps`, `top`, `kill`, and `nice`, you gain the ability to monitor, control, and optimize your system's processes. The more you interact with processes, the more you'll realize that they are the heart of a Unix system—without processes, nothing would get done. By gaining an understanding of how they operate and how to manage them, you'll be better equipped to keep your system running smoothly and efficiently.

22. To wrap up, remember that processes in Unix are not just individual programs; they are the building blocks of everything your system does. Each command you run is a process, and each process plays a role in the system's overall operation. Whether you're managing system resources, optimizing performance, or debugging issues, having a strong grasp of how processes work and how to manage them will be one of the most valuable skills you can acquire. So keep experimenting with these commands, and soon, you'll feel like the true master of your Unix system, controlling the magic happening behind the scenes with ease.

As you continue to explore processes in Unix, you'll encounter more complex concepts, such as **background jobs**, **suspending and resuming processes**, and **process signals**. Let's dive a bit deeper into each of these.

First, let's talk about **background jobs** and how to manage them. When you run a process in the background, as you've seen with the & symbol, it allows you to continue using your terminal for other tasks while the process runs. But what if you've already started a long-running process and you want to move it to the background? You can suspend it by pressing `Ctrl + Z`, which will stop the process temporarily and place it into the background as a suspended job. To see a list of all background and suspended jobs, you can use the `jobs` command. If you want to send a suspended job to the background and have it run without blocking your terminal, simply use the `bg` command followed by the job number:

bash
Copy
```
bg %1
```
This sends job 1 to the background to run as a background job. If you want to bring a background job back to the foreground, you can use the `fg` command:

bash
Copy
```
fg %1
```

Managing background jobs is useful when you're multitasking in the terminal and need to run several processes at once without blocking your workflow.

Now, let's discuss **process signals**—a vital concept when it comes to process management. In Unix, processes can receive signals that tell them to perform certain actions. Signals are essentially messages sent by the system or other processes that instruct the process to do something, such as terminate, pause, or continue. The most common signal is SIGTERM, which asks a process to terminate gracefully. Another commonly used signal is SIGKILL, which forcefully kills a process without allowing it to clean up. You can send a signal to a process using the kill command, which might sound harsh, but it's a necessary tool when dealing with processes that are misbehaving. For example, to send a SIGTERM to a process, you can run:

bash
Copy
```
kill PID
```
If the process refuses to terminate, you can use SIGKILL by appending -9 to the command:

bash
Copy
```
kill -9 PID
```
This will immediately terminate the process without giving it a chance to clean up. Other useful signals include SIGSTOP to stop a process (pause it) and SIGCONT to resume a process that's been paused.

Sometimes, you might want to check the **status** or **state** of a running process, particularly if it's taking longer than expected or seems to be stuck. Unix provides the ps and top commands for this, but you can also use the strace command to trace system calls and signals. This is especially useful when you're debugging or investigating processes that aren't behaving as expected. For example:

bash
Copy
```
strace -p PID
```
This will show you the system calls that the process is making, giving you insight into what it's doing behind the scenes. strace is an incredibly useful tool for diagnosing issues with processes, such as when a process is stuck waiting for input or trying to access a file.

One aspect of processes you might encounter, especially in multi-user environments, is **process prioritization**. As mentioned earlier, Unix allows you to change the priority of a process using the nice and renice commands. The priority of a process determines how much CPU time it gets in relation to other processes. A process with a higher priority will receive more CPU time, while a process with a lower priority will be starved of resources. This is where the nice command comes in handy: if you want to start a process with a lower priority, you can use:

```bash
Copy
nice -n 10 command
```
This sets the priority of the process to a lower level (10 in this case). If you want to increase the priority of a running process, you can use the `renice` command:

```bash
Copy
renice -n -5 -p PID
```
This will increase the priority of the process with the given PID by changing its `nice` value. Prioritizing processes ensures that critical tasks get the resources they need, while less important tasks don't hog the system.

Now, consider the **zombie** processes. These are processes that have completed their execution but still appear in the process table because their parent process hasn't yet read their exit status. These "dead" processes are no longer running but occupy a small amount of system resources. While they don't consume CPU, they can accumulate over time if the parent process doesn't clean them up properly. To check for zombie processes, use `ps aux | grep Z` — this will show processes in the "Z" (zombie) state. Normally, zombie processes are automatically cleaned up, but if they pile up, you might need to manually terminate the parent process or restart the system to clear them out.

Another helpful tool for monitoring processes is the **pstree** command. Unlike `ps`, which shows processes in a list format, `pstree` shows processes in a tree-like structure, allowing you to visualize the parent-child relationships between processes. This makes it easy to see which processes were spawned by other processes and which processes are consuming the most resources. For example:

```bash
Copy
pstree
```
This will display the process tree starting from the init process, showing all the running processes and their relationships. `pstree` is an excellent tool for understanding how processes are related and which ones are active at any given time.

As you become more comfortable with processes, you'll start to appreciate how Unix uses **process groups** and **sessions** to manage related processes. A **process group** is a set of processes that are related to one another, and they can be managed collectively. A **session** is a collection of process groups, typically tied to a single user or terminal session. These concepts are essential when you're working with multiple processes that need to be controlled together—like when running a series of commands in a script or managing jobs in the background.

If you're managing many processes and jobs, using **job control** will be essential. Job control in Unix allows you to start, stop, and manage background jobs interactively. The `fg`, `bg`, `jobs`, `kill`, and `Ctrl + Z` shortcuts are all part of this system. Understanding how to suspend and resume jobs, as well as manage background tasks, will make multitasking in the terminal much more efficient.

In summary, processes are a fundamental part of any Unix-based operating system. They are what allow you to interact with the system, run commands, and perform tasks. Understanding processes gives you a deeper insight into how Unix works behind the scenes and helps you manage your system more efficiently. From viewing processes with `ps` to managing their priority with `nice`, terminating processes with `kill`, and even debugging them with `strace`, you now have the tools to control processes at your fingertips. As you continue your Unix journey, the ability to manage processes efficiently will be one of your most powerful skills.

The next time you run a command and wonder what's happening behind the scenes, you'll have a much clearer picture. You'll know how processes are created, how they interact, how to prioritize them, and how to control them. With this knowledge, you'll be able to troubleshoot system performance issues, optimize resource usage, and keep your system running smoothly. Unix is a multitasking powerhouse, and with a strong understanding of processes, you'll be able to harness its full potential. So, take the time to explore and experiment with process management, because the more you understand processes, the more control you'll have over your Unix system.

Chapter 10: Power to the Users: Creating and Managing Accounts

1. In the world of Unix, users are at the heart of everything. Whether you're working on your own personal computer or managing a multi-user system, understanding how to create and manage user accounts is crucial for both security and efficiency. Users are the lifeblood of any Unix system, each having their own unique permissions and access to files and resources. In this chapter, we're going to explore the world of **user management** in Unix, from creating new users to managing their permissions, and everything in between. By the end of this chapter, you'll have a solid understanding of how to create, modify, and secure user accounts, empowering you to maintain a Unix system where only the right people have access to the right resources.

2. Let's start with the **basics** of user accounts in Unix. When you install a Unix-based system, the installation process typically creates a **root** account, which has superuser privileges, and possibly a default user account. Every other user you create has a unique username and associated ID (UID). Users are typically grouped together in **user groups**, which simplify the management of permissions and access control. Groups are collections of users who share the same access rights, and you can assign multiple users to a group based on their roles or needs. Users have their own **home directories**, typically located in `/home/username`, where they can store personal files and data. Each user also has a set of **permissions** that govern what files and resources they can access.

3. Now that we've covered the basics, let's talk about how to create a **new user**. The `useradd` command is the primary tool for creating new users on a Unix system. To create a simple user account, you'd run the following command:

bash
Copy

```
sudo useradd username
```

4.

This command creates a new user with the username `username`, but it doesn't set up a home directory or password by default. To create a user with a home directory and default configuration, you can use the `-m` option:

bash
Copy

```
sudo useradd -m username
```

5.

This ensures that a home directory is created in `/home/username`. After creating the user, you'll also need to set a password for the new account using the `passwd` command:

bash
Copy

```
sudo passwd username
```

6.

This will prompt you to enter a new password for the user. Once the password is set, the new user can log in with their credentials.

7. Along with creating users, you'll often need to assign them to one or more **user groups**. Groups allow you to organize users based on their roles and grant them permissions collectively. To add a user to a specific group, you can use the `usermod` command. For example, to add `username` to the `admin` group, you'd run:

bash

```
sudo usermod -aG admin username
```

8.

The **-aG** flag tells **usermod** to add the user to the specified group without removing them from any other groups they belong to. Groups are a powerful tool for managing access to shared resources—rather than assigning permissions to individual users, you can assign them to groups and manage access at a higher level.

9. In addition to creating users and assigning them to groups, you'll also want to manage **user information**. Each user in Unix has a set of associated information, such as their full name, contact information, and default shell. You can modify this information using the **usermod** command. For example, if you want to change the user's shell, you can use:
bash

```
sudo usermod -s /bin/bash username
```

10.

This changes the default shell for the user to **/bin/bash**. You can also modify other details, such as the user's home directory or full name, with similar flags. To view the current information for a user, you can check the **/etc/passwd** file, which contains all the details about each user account, such as the username, UID, GID (group ID), home directory, and shell.

11. Another useful tool for managing users is the **groupadd** command, which allows you to create new groups. To create a new group called **developers**, you would run:
bash

```
sudo groupadd developers
```

12.

Once the group is created, you can add users to it using the `usermod` command as we discussed earlier. Groups make it easier to manage permissions for a group of users who need access to the same resources, such as shared directories or files. You can view the groups a user belongs to by using the `groups` command:

bash
Copy

```
groups username
```

13.

This will display all the groups the user is a part of, allowing you to easily track their access rights.

14. As a system administrator, it's important to **delete users** when they're no longer needed, or when they leave the organization. The `userdel` command allows you to remove a user from the system. For example:

bash
Copy

```
sudo userdel username
```

15.

This will remove the user's account, but it will **not** remove their home directory or files by default. To delete the user along with their home directory and files, use the `-r` option:

bash
Copy

```
sudo userdel -r username
```

16.

Be cautious when deleting users, as this action is irreversible and can result in the loss of important data. Always ensure that you've backed up any critical files before removing a user.

17. Managing **user permissions** is a critical part of maintaining a secure system. Each user has a set of permissions that control their access to files and resources. These permissions

can be modified using the chmod command, but user-specific access is typically managed through **groups** and the files they own. For example, the chmod command allows you to grant or revoke read, write, and execute permissions for a file or directory. For example, to allow a user to read and write to a file but not execute it, you would run:

bash
Copy

```
chmod u+rw file.txt
```

18.

Understanding how to manage user permissions is essential for preventing unauthorized access to sensitive files and ensuring that each user has the right level of access to resources.

19. In multi-user environments, it's also essential to keep track of **inactive users**. Unix provides the chage command, which allows you to set user password expiration policies and manage account inactivity. For example, you can set a user's password to expire after 30 days by running:

bash
Copy

```
sudo chage -M 30 username
```

20.

This will force the user to change their password every 30 days. You can also set an account to expire after a certain date, effectively disabling the user's login ability. This is useful for enforcing security policies and ensuring that old accounts don't remain active when they are no longer needed.

21. Another critical aspect of user management is understanding **sudo** (superuser do) privileges. The sudo command allows users to run commands with elevated privileges, temporarily granting them access to perform tasks typically reserved for the root user. By default, only users in the sudo or wheel group have access to sudo on most Unix systems. You can grant or revoke sudo privileges for users by adding them to the appropriate group or editing the /etc/sudoers file. To add a user to the sudo group, you would use:

bash
Copy

```
sudo usermod -aG sudo username
```

22.

This is a great way to allow certain users to perform administrative tasks without giving them full root access. Always be cautious when granting `sudo` privileges, as it gives users the ability to make system-wide changes.

23. A very important aspect of managing users is **security**. Protecting user accounts and preventing unauthorized access is essential for keeping your system safe. Some best practices include setting strong passwords, using two-factor authentication (if possible), and regularly reviewing and auditing user accounts. It's also important to monitor login activity and check for any unusual or unauthorized access attempts. You can check the system's authentication logs by reviewing files like `/var/log/auth.log` (or `/var/log/secure` on some distributions). Regularly auditing your user accounts and permissions helps maintain a secure environment.

24. Managing **user quotas** is another important aspect of maintaining a multi-user Unix system. In a multi-user environment, it's essential to prevent any user from consuming all of the available disk space. With disk quotas, you can limit the amount of disk space each user can use. You can configure and manage quotas using commands like `quota`, `edquota`, and `repquota`. These tools allow you to set soft and hard limits on user disk usage, helping prevent any one user from overwhelming the system resources.

25. In conclusion, managing users is a fundamental skill for anyone working with Unix. By understanding how to create, modify, and delete user accounts, assign groups, manage permissions, and implement security measures, you'll ensure that your system is both secure and efficient. Whether you're running a single-user desktop or a multi-user server, proper user management will help you control access, keep your system organized, and maintain security. With these tools at your disposal, you can give the right users the right access and keep your system running smoothly.

One more important aspect of user management is **user account locking**. In certain situations, you might need to temporarily disable a user account, whether for maintenance, security reasons, or because the user is no longer actively using the system. Unix provides tools to lock and unlock user accounts easily. You can lock a user account by using the `passwd` command with the `-l` option:

```bash
Copy
sudo passwd -l username
```

This will disable the user's password, effectively preventing them from logging in. If you want to unlock the account later, you can use the −u option:

```bash
```
Copy
```
sudo passwd -u username
```
Account locking is particularly useful for administrators who need to temporarily disable a user's access without fully deleting their account.

Another important tool for managing user accounts in a Unix environment is **LDAP (Lightweight Directory Access Protocol)**. LDAP allows you to manage user accounts across multiple machines by centralizing the user data. This is especially useful for organizations with large numbers of users or systems. With LDAP, you can authenticate users and manage their access rights from a single server, making it easier to enforce consistent security policies. While LDAP is beyond the scope of basic user management, it's worth knowing that it can be integrated into Unix systems for large-scale user management.

As you manage users, you'll also want to be aware of **system users**. These are special accounts that the system uses for running services or background processes, rather than for human interaction. For example, the root account is a system user with full administrative access to the system. Other system users include those used for running web servers (such as www-data for Apache), databases, and other background services. These accounts typically have limited permissions to reduce security risks. You can list all users on the system by looking at the /etc/passwd file, which contains both human and system accounts. When creating new users, be sure to differentiate between human users (who need home directories and interactive logins) and system users (who don't).

Auditing user activities is another critical step in maintaining a secure and well-managed Unix system. Regularly checking who is logged in, what they are doing, and how long they have been active is crucial for monitoring system security. Commands like w, who, and last can provide insight into user activities. For example, w displays information about the users currently logged into the system and what they are doing:

```bash
```
Copy
```
w
```
Similarly, last shows the last login times for users, which is useful for auditing and tracking login patterns. Regularly reviewing these logs and monitoring user activity helps detect unauthorized access or suspicious behavior.

One additional security measure you should be aware of is **sudo logging**. When users execute commands with sudo, the actions they take are logged to /var/log/auth.log (or /var/log/secure on some systems). This log keeps a record of which commands were executed with elevated privileges and by whom. Regularly reviewing these logs is a good practice for system administrators to ensure that there are no unauthorized or suspicious activities involving elevated permissions. You can monitor sudo usage with the `sudo` command's built-in logging, but also consider using tools like `auditd` for more advanced auditing capabilities.

To wrap things up, managing users in Unix involves more than just creating accounts. It's about keeping track of who has access to what, maintaining security, and ensuring that your system runs smoothly for everyone involved. From creating and modifying accounts with `useradd` and `usermod` to managing groups, permissions, and security settings, you now have the tools to effectively manage a Unix system. Whether you're an individual user setting up your personal account or an administrator managing hundreds of accounts in a large organization, understanding user management is essential for maintaining a secure and efficient system.

Remember, as you continue to work with user accounts, always consider security as a top priority. Limit access to sensitive resources, use strong passwords, and regularly audit user activity. Utilize the right tools and commands to create and manage user accounts, ensuring that only authorized users have the appropriate level of access. By mastering user management in Unix, you'll not only ensure the security and organization of your system, but you'll also be better equipped to handle issues as they arise. Proper user management is the cornerstone of a well-maintained, secure, and efficient Unix environment, and you now have the skills to implement it effectively.

Lastly, always be proactive when it comes to managing accounts. Regularly review user access, ensure that old accounts are removed or locked when no longer in use, and enforce best practices for password policies. A good Unix administrator not only knows how to create and delete accounts but also understands the importance of maintaining a secure, organized, and manageable system. As you continue to gain experience with Unix, user management will become second nature, and you'll be able to keep your system running securely and smoothly.

So, take a moment to practice these commands and techniques in your own Unix environment. Create test accounts, modify their settings, and practice managing their permissions. With these tools in hand, you'll be ready to tackle any user management challenge that comes your way, ensuring that your Unix system is always in good hands.

Congratulations on mastering the art of user management in Unix! This chapter has equipped you with the essential knowledge needed to control access, maintain security, and effectively manage users on your system. Whether you're configuring your own personal system or overseeing a multi-user environment, you now have the skills to handle the demands of user management confidently. So, keep practicing, keep learning, and continue to build your Unix expertise—because in the world of Unix, managing users is where the power truly lies!

Chapter 11: The Unix Family: Working with System Services

1. Behind every smooth-running Unix system is a collection of **system services**, also known as **daemons**, that keep everything ticking along in the background. These services are responsible for everything from managing networking and handling web traffic to scheduling tasks and ensuring security. You may not always see these services at work,

but they're running all the time, doing the heavy lifting that makes your system functional. In this chapter, we're going to explore the world of system services in Unix. You'll learn how to start, stop, and manage these services, troubleshoot issues, and configure them to meet your needs. Understanding how system services work is crucial for any Unix user or administrator, whether you're managing a personal machine or a large-scale server.

2. First, let's get familiar with what a **system service** is. In Unix, services are usually **background processes**—programs that run without direct interaction from the user. These services, or daemons, are initiated by the system at boot time or manually by the user or system administrator. For example, the Apache web server (`httpd`), the SSH service (`sshd`), and cron jobs (for scheduling tasks) are all examples of system services. These processes run with elevated privileges, ensuring that the system has access to the resources it needs to operate effectively. Some services might be constantly running, while others might only activate in response to specific events, such as a user request or a scheduled task.

3. To view the system services currently running on your Unix machine, the `ps` command is a great tool to start with. Running `ps aux` will show you a list of all processes running on your system, including system services. You can filter this list further by using the `grep` command to search for specific services. For example, if you want to check if the SSH service is running, you can use:

```bash
Copy


ps aux | grep sshd
```

4.

This command will display any processes related to `sshd`, the SSH daemon. If it's running, you'll see its process in the output. If it's not running, the command won't return anything, which tells you that the service is inactive.

5. While `ps` is great for viewing processes, it's not the best tool for managing them. For managing system services, **systemd** (on systems that use it) or **init** (on older systems) are the primary systems responsible for starting, stopping, and monitoring services. `systemd` is the default system and service manager for many modern Linux distributions, while older Unix systems may still rely on `init` scripts to manage services. In this chapter, we'll primarily focus on `systemd`, as it's now the most common method for managing services.

6. To interact with services managed by `systemd`, you'll use the `systemctl` command. This is the go-to command for starting, stopping, and controlling system

services. The basic syntax for controlling a service looks like this:
bash
Copy

```
sudo systemctl start service-name
```

7.

For example, to start the SSH service, you would run:
bash
Copy

```
sudo systemctl start sshd
```

8.

This starts the SSH daemon (`sshd`) and allows SSH connections to your system. Similarly, you can stop a service with:
bash
Copy

```
sudo systemctl stop service-name
```

9.

To restart a service, use:
bash
Copy

```
sudo systemctl restart service-name
```

10.

And to check the status of a service (whether it's running or not), you can use:
bash
Copy

```bash
sudo systemctl status service-name
```

11.

12. One of the most important aspects of system services is **enabling** and **disabling** them at startup. When you enable a service, you tell the system to start that service automatically every time the system boots. To enable a service, use:
bash
Copy

```bash
sudo systemctl enable service-name
```

13.

For example, to ensure that the SSH service starts automatically every time the system boots, you can run:
bash
Copy

```bash
sudo systemctl enable sshd
```

14.

Conversely, if you want to prevent a service from starting automatically, you can disable it with:
bash
Copy

```bash
sudo systemctl disable service-name
```

15.

16. Sometimes, you might need to **mask** a service, which is a more extreme form of disabling it. Masking a service ensures that it cannot be started, either manually or automatically, and is often used for security purposes when you want to prevent a service from being launched under any circumstances. To mask a service, use:

```bash
Copy
```

```bash
sudo systemctl mask service-name
```

17.

To unmask a service (so that it can be started again), use:

```bash
Copy
```

```bash
sudo systemctl unmask service-name
```

18.

19. In addition to `systemd`, some systems still rely on traditional **init.d scripts** to manage system services. These scripts are usually stored in `/etc/init.d/` and can be used to start or stop services in older Unix systems. While `systemd` has largely replaced `init.d` scripts in modern Linux distributions, you may encounter them in older systems or on Unix-like systems such as macOS. To start or stop a service using `init.d` scripts, you would run:

```bash
Copy
```

```bash
sudo /etc/init.d/service-name start
```

20. `sudo /etc/init.d/service-name stop`
21.

The `init.d` approach isn't as flexible as `systemd`, but it still works on many systems for basic service management.
22. Sometimes, services don't start properly, and you'll need to troubleshoot the issue. One of the first places to check when a service fails to start is its **log files**. System services generally log their activity to system log files, which you can access with the `journalctl` command if you're using `systemd`. For example, to see the logs for the SSH service, you can run:

```bash
```

```
sudo journalctl -u sshd
```

23.

This will show you the logs related to the `sshd` service, which can help you diagnose why the service might not be starting or why it's behaving incorrectly. You can also check the general system logs, which are typically stored in `/var/log/` and can be viewed using tools like `cat`, `less`, or `tail`.

24. Another useful tool for service troubleshooting is **systemctl status**. Not only does it show whether a service is running, but it also includes useful log messages that may point to the problem. If a service has failed to start, `systemctl status` will usually show an error message or status code that helps pinpoint what went wrong. For example:

bash

```
sudo systemctl status sshd
```

25.

This will show the current status of the `sshd` service and provide any error messages related to its startup. If a service fails, these status messages can give you a starting point for fixing the issue.

26. It's also worth mentioning that many services run as **background processes** or **daemons**, and they can often be managed through the system's built-in process management system. If you're unsure whether a service is running, you can use commands like `ps`, `top`, or `htop` to check for the service's processes. For example:

bash

```
ps aux | grep sshd
```

27.

This shows you all the processes related to the `sshd` service. If the service is running, you'll see it listed here. If it's not, you can use the `systemctl` or `init.d` commands to start it.

28. A key concept in service management is **service dependencies**. Some services rely on other services to function properly. For example, the web server (`apache2`) might depend on the networking service being up and running. With `systemd`, you can view service dependencies with the `systemctl list-dependencies` command. For example:

bash
Copy

```
sudo systemctl list-dependencies apache2
```

29.

This will list all of the services that `apache2` depends on, and you can use this information to ensure that all the necessary services are running before you attempt to start your service.

30. Finally, let's touch on **systemd targets**. Targets are like runlevels in older Unix systems — they define the state of the system, specifying which services should be running at a given time. Some common targets include `multi-user.target`, which is equivalent to the traditional runlevel 3, and `graphical.target`, which is used for systems with a graphical interface. You can switch between targets using `systemctl`:

bash
Copy

```
sudo systemctl isolate graphical.target
```

31.

This command switches the system to graphical mode (if available). Targets are useful for managing the overall state of the system and ensuring that only the necessary services are running.

32. In conclusion, system services are an integral part of any Unix-based system. They are the unsung heroes that run in the background, providing all the essential services that make your system function smoothly. Whether you're using `systemd` to manage services, troubleshooting with `journalctl`, or adjusting system targets, understanding how to work with services will give you the control and flexibility to

optimize your system. By mastering service management, you'll be able to ensure that your system is always running the services it needs and not wasting resources on unnecessary ones. So, whether you're an administrator managing servers or a user trying to troubleshoot a service, knowing how to work with system services is a vital skill in your Unix toolkit. Happy service managing!

As we wrap up this chapter, it's important to recognize how central **system services** are to maintaining and troubleshooting your Unix system. Understanding how to control, monitor, and troubleshoot these services will make you far more effective as a user or administrator. Whether you're dealing with essential services like networking, SSH, or cron jobs, or you're adding new daemons to your system, the key to managing these services effectively lies in knowing the tools at your disposal—commands like `systemctl`, `ps`, `journalctl`, and `top` are your allies in ensuring smooth operation.

It's also worth noting that **security** plays a huge role in managing services. Each service runs with specific permissions, often as its own user or group, and has access to certain system resources. Ensuring that services are correctly configured and secured is critical for keeping your system safe from malicious attacks. One of the best ways to secure services is by running only the services you need. Disable unnecessary services and use firewall rules to limit access to those that are necessary. Additionally, for services that involve remote access, such as SSH, it's essential to configure them properly to avoid vulnerabilities, such as brute-force login attempts. Always keep an eye on log files for any suspicious activity, as they can often reveal early signs of an issue.

If you're working on a **server** or multi-user environment, knowing how to manage user access to services is a huge part of maintaining both security and efficiency. For example, when you're managing a web server, you'll want to ensure that the web service has restricted access to only certain resources and directories. You can manage this with file permissions, groups, and by configuring the service's own user, ensuring that it has the least privileges necessary to function. Many services also have configuration files that can be edited to control access, and understanding these files is key to proper system management.

Service management also plays a vital role in **system automation**. By creating service-specific configuration files or scripts, you can automate many system tasks such as backups, log rotation, and regular updates. Automating the start-up of services or scheduled tasks with tools like `cron` allows you to reduce manual intervention and ensure that critical services start up automatically after a reboot. This reduces the risk of human error and ensures that services are consistently running when needed.

One useful aspect of `systemd` is its **service unit files**. These configuration files allow you to control how services start, stop, and behave at boot time. They define dependencies, startup ordering, and service behavior, and you can create your own custom unit files for services that are not managed by the default system. For example, you can create a custom service to manage a script or a program that should run at startup. To do this, you would write a unit file for the service, typically stored in `/etc/systemd/system/`. Once the unit file is created, you can enable and manage your custom service just like any other service managed by `systemd`.

While `systemd` is the most commonly used service manager in modern Unix-like systems, it's important to know that **other systems** (like BSD or macOS) may use different methods to handle services. For example, BSD systems use the **rc.d** script system for starting and stopping services, and macOS uses launchd. These systems still follow similar concepts but may have different tools and commands. As you work across different Unix systems, understanding how these systems handle services will help you maintain a consistent workflow.

For advanced users and administrators, **service monitoring and performance** become crucial aspects of managing system services. Services that consume excessive resources or fail to respond can severely impact the performance of your system. Tools like `top`, `htop`, and `atop` are useful for monitoring resource usage in real-time. By keeping track of CPU, memory, and disk I/O usage, you can quickly identify resource hogs and take action before they disrupt the system. Additionally, integrating performance monitoring tools such as `Prometheus` or `Nagios` can help you set up alerts and notifications to proactively manage system performance.

Regular updates and **patching** of system services are essential for keeping your system secure and running smoothly. Security vulnerabilities are discovered frequently in software, including system services. By keeping services up to date with the latest patches, you help prevent attackers from exploiting these vulnerabilities. Many package managers, such as `apt` on Debian-based systems or `yum` on RedHat-based systems, offer the ability to update system services along with their dependencies. Automated tools can help ensure that your system services are regularly checked and updated to avoid any security holes.

A crucial part of managing system services is knowing when to **restart** them. Sometimes, services require a restart to apply configuration changes or to recover from errors. While it's always possible to stop and start services manually, you can streamline this with the `systemctl` restart command, which will handle both stopping and starting the service in one go. For example:

bash
Copy
```
sudo systemctl restart apache2
```
This command is handy when you change configuration files and need to reload them without rebooting the entire system. However, if a service is continuously failing, it's worth checking its logs and system status first to understand why it's misbehaving, as repeated restarts might just mask the underlying issue.

Lastly, understanding **service dependencies** is key to managing complex systems. Services don't exist in isolation; some require other services to be running in order to function correctly. With `systemd`, you can view the dependencies for any service by using the `systemctl list-dependencies` command. For example:

bash
Copy
```
sudo systemctl list-dependencies apache2
```

This will show you all services that need to be running in order for `apache2` to function. Being aware of service dependencies can help you troubleshoot issues when a service fails to start or behaves unexpectedly. It's important to ensure that required services are up and running, and that no conflicting services are taking up resources.

In conclusion, system services are the foundation of a Unix system's functionality. They run silently in the background, but they are essential for everything from networking and web services to security and automation. By learning how to control, monitor, and troubleshoot these services, you'll gain a deeper understanding of how Unix operates and how to keep it running smoothly. Whether you're managing essential services like SSH and Apache or dealing with custom services specific to your system, knowing how to work with system services will make you a more efficient and effective Unix user. So take the time to learn the tools and best practices for service management, and you'll be well-equipped to handle any service-related challenges that come your way.

Chapter 12: Searching for Treasure: Finding Files Like a Pro

1. If you've ever found yourself lost in a sea of files on your Unix system, trying to locate that one elusive document, you know how frustrating it can be. But fear not! In this chapter, we're going to explore the powerful tools and techniques Unix provides to help you search for files like a pro. Whether you're looking for a specific file by name, searching for content inside files, or locating files based on their size or modification date, Unix has the tools you need to uncover your digital treasure. Get ready to unlock the secrets of searching and find your way around any file system with ease.

2. Let's start with one of the most fundamental commands for finding files: **find**. The `find` command is the Swiss Army knife of file searching in Unix. It allows you to search directories and subdirectories for files that match specific criteria, such as name, type, size, or modification time. For example, if you want to find a file named `report.txt` in your home directory, you can use:
    bash
    Copy

```
find ~ -name "report.txt"
```

3.

    This command starts searching from your home directory (~) and looks for any file named `report.txt`. The `-name` option specifies that you're looking for files that match the name you've provided. You can also use wildcards with `find` to search for files that match a pattern. For example, to find all `.txt` files, you can run:
    bash

```
find ~ -name "*.txt"
```

4.

The asterisk (`*`) acts as a wildcard that matches any string of characters. This is just the beginning of what `find` can do!

5. The `find` command is incredibly versatile, allowing you to search for files based on a wide range of criteria. Want to find files that were modified within the last 7 days? Use the `-mtime` option:

bash

```
find ~ -mtime -7
```

6.

This will list all files modified in the last 7 days. You can also use `-mtime +7` to find files modified more than 7 days ago. The `-ctime` option works similarly, but it searches for files based on when their metadata (such as permissions or ownership) was last changed. For even more control, the `-size` option allows you to search for files of a specific size, like this:

bash

```
find ~ -size +10M
```

7.

This command will find all files larger than 10 megabytes. The possibilities are endless— `find` is an indispensable tool for locating files based on just about any criterion.

8. But what if you don't just need to find a file by name or date, but you want to search inside the files themselves for specific content? This is where **grep** comes into play. The `grep` command allows you to search for specific patterns inside files. It's like a treasure map that leads you to hidden content. For example, if you want to search for the word "error" inside all `.log` files in the current directory, you can use:

```bash
Copy


grep "error" *.log
```

9.

This will print out all lines containing the word "error" from any `.log` file in the current directory. You can even search recursively through all subdirectories using the `-r` flag:

```bash
Copy


grep -r "error" /path/to/directory
```

10.

This will search through all files in the specified directory and its subdirectories for the word "error". `grep` is a powerful tool for finding specific content within files, and it's an essential part of any Unix user's toolkit.

11. While `grep` is great for searching text within files, sometimes you need to search for files containing specific content based on more complex patterns. For this, `grep` supports **regular expressions**—a powerful way to define search patterns. Regular expressions allow you to search for complex patterns, such as matching any word that starts with "err" (like "error", "erroneous", or "erratic"):

```bash
Copy


grep -r "^err" /path/to/directory
```

12.

This command will search for any line that begins with "err". Regular expressions are incredibly powerful, and once you learn how to use them, you'll be able to search for virtually any pattern in your files.

13. Another useful tool for locating files based on their contents is **locate**. The `locate` command allows you to search for files by name, but it does so much faster than `find` because it relies on an indexed database of file paths. For example, to find all files

containing "report" in their name, you can run:

```bash
locate report
```

14.

This will return a list of all file paths that contain the word "report". The catch is that the `locate` database isn't always up-to-date—it's refreshed periodically through a cron job or can be updated manually with the `updatedb` command. While `locate` is incredibly fast, you should use it knowing that its results may not reflect files created or moved since the last database update.

15. If you're working with a large file system and you're looking for a quick way to find files based on **file types**, the `find` command can help here as well. Using the `-type` option, you can search for specific types of files. For example, if you want to find all directories, you can use:

```bash
find ~ -type d
```

16.

This command searches for directories (`d` stands for directory). If you want to search for regular files, use `-type f`. You can also search for symbolic links (`-type l`), sockets (`-type s`), and other file types. This is incredibly useful when you're narrowing down your search and need to focus on a specific type of file.

17. Sometimes, you might want to search for files **modified recently** or files that have **not been accessed** in a while. In addition to `find` and `grep`, Unix provides the `stat` command to gather detailed information about a file, including its access, modification, and change times. To view the detailed stats for a file, run:

```bash
stat filename
```

18.

The output will show you when the file was last accessed, modified, and changed. This is helpful for investigating file history, especially if you're troubleshooting or auditing system activity.

19. Let's not forget about **file name expansion** and **wildcards**, which can make your searches much more efficient. Wildcards like `*`, `?`, and `[ ]` can be used to match groups of files. For example:

- `*` matches any number of characters (e.g., `*.txt` will match all files with a `.txt` extension).

- `?` matches a single character (e.g., `file?.txt` will match `file1.txt`, `fileA.txt`, etc.).

- `[ ]` matches a range of characters (e.g., `file[1-5].txt` will match `file1.txt`, `file2.txt`, etc.).

20. You can use these wildcards with commands like `find` and `ls` to quickly locate files that match patterns without needing to specify the exact name. This is a great way to work with groups of files that follow a naming convention.

21. For **advanced searching** across file systems, Unix also allows you to use **indexing tools** to speed up file searches. Tools like **mlocate** (an improved version of `locate`) provide faster search results by indexing your file system. The key advantage of using an indexing tool is that it can provide near-instant results for searches across large file systems. The trade-off is that, just like `locate`, these tools rely on an index that needs to be regularly updated.

22. Once you get used to searching for files, you'll want to start learning how to **combine search results**. Unix provides several tools that can help you manipulate and format search results. For instance, the `find` command can be combined with `exec` to perform actions on the files it locates. For example, if you want to find all `.txt` files and then delete them, you can run:
bash
Copy

```
find ~ -name "*.txt" -exec rm {} \;
```

23.

The `{ }` placeholder represents the files found, and the `\ ;` indicates the end of the command. This is just one example of how you can automate actions based on search results. `find` can be combined with other commands to perform actions like moving, copying, or modifying files.

24. Searching for files efficiently is one of the most powerful skills in Unix. Whether you're hunting for a single file, locating content inside files, filtering by specific attributes, or automating tasks based on search results, the tools we've discussed—`find`, `grep`, `locate`, and their companions—are indispensable. With these tools, you'll be able to search your file system like a pro, pinpointing exactly what you need in seconds, even on a sprawling Unix server.

25. So, the next time you find yourself in need of a lost file, remember that Unix has a treasure trove of powerful commands at your disposal to help you track it down. Mastering the art of searching in Unix will save you countless hours and give you confidence in navigating even the most complex systems. From using wildcards to leveraging regular expressions and beyond, you're now equipped with everything you need to find your way to the files you're looking for—like a pro. Happy hunting!

Once you've mastered basic file searching, you can take it a step further by **automating searches** and combining them with other system commands to create even more powerful workflows. One excellent tool for this is the **xargs** command. **xargs** takes input from a command (like `find`) and passes it as arguments to another command, which allows you to chain multiple operations together. For example, if you want to find all `.log` files in a directory and then compress them using `gzip`, you could run:

bash
Copy
```bash
find ~ -name "*.log" | xargs gzip
```
Here, `find` locates all `.log` files, and `xargs` takes each file and passes it to `gzip` for compression. This is a simple but powerful way to automate tasks, especially when dealing with a large number of files.

Another way to automate searches and create custom workflows is through **scripting**. If you find yourself regularly searching for files with the same criteria, you can write a script that performs these searches automatically. For example, you might write a script to search for any `.log` files older than 30 days, delete them, and then send a notification:

bash
Copy
```bash
#!/bin/bash
find ~ -name "*.log" -mtime +30 -exec rm {} \;
echo "Old log files deleted."
```

This script automates the entire process, saving you time and ensuring that you don't forget to perform routine file management tasks. Scripting is an incredibly powerful feature of Unix that allows you to create custom solutions for your everyday tasks.

If you're working with **large datasets** or **logs**, sometimes it's not just about finding files but about efficiently **processing the results**. Unix provides a wealth of tools for this, such as `awk`, `sed`, and `cut`. For example, say you're searching through a large log file for all lines containing "error," and you want to display only the fifth column from the results. You can combine `grep` and `awk` like this:

bash
Copy
```bash
grep "error" /var/log/system.log | awk '{print $5}'
```
This command filters the log file for "error" and then uses `awk` to print the fifth column from each matching line. By combining search and text processing tools, you can extract exactly the information you need from large, complex files.

Handling symbolic links in searches is another essential skill. When using `find` to search for files, you may want to ignore or follow symbolic links (symlinks) depending on your needs. By default, `find` will follow symlinks, but you can prevent this behavior with the `-P` flag (to avoid following symlinks) or use `-L` to follow symlinks explicitly. For example, if you only want to find **regular files** and not symlinks, you can use:

bash
Copy
```bash
find ~ -type f -P
```
This command ensures that `find` only returns regular files and avoids symlinks. Similarly, if you need to follow symlinks and search the files they point to, you can use the `-L` option:

bash
Copy
```bash
find ~ -type f -L
```
Understanding how to deal with symlinks in your searches will help you avoid issues like counting symlinks as regular files or missing files linked to other locations.

Another powerful tool for searching and managing large directories or datasets is **fd**—a modern alternative to `find`. `fd` is faster, easier to use, and provides better default behavior for many common search tasks. For example, to search for all `.txt` files in your home directory, you would simply run:

bash
Copy
```bash
fd "*.txt" ~
```

The beauty of `fd` is that it automatically ignores hidden directories (like `.git`), and it has built-in regular expression support, making searches more intuitive and efficient. If you haven't tried `fd`, it's definitely worth installing and adding to your toolbox for file searching.

File indexing and search utilities like `locate` are incredibly useful for quick searches, but they require periodic updates to their index. If you're working with real-time systems or data that changes frequently, you might find `locate` to be less reliable unless it's regularly updated. The `updatedb` command can be used to manually update the index:

bash
Copy
```
sudo updatedb
```
Running `updatedb` will refresh the database used by `locate`, ensuring that future searches reflect the most current state of the file system. For systems that are constantly adding or modifying files, consider automating this update process or setting it up as a cron job to ensure the index is always up-to-date.

Let's take a moment to highlight **search efficiency**. If you're searching through a vast file system, the way you structure your searches can greatly impact how quickly results are returned. Always start by narrowing down your search to the specific directory or range of files you're interested in. For example, rather than searching your entire home directory, focus on specific subdirectories to avoid unnecessary overhead. If you are searching large directories, consider limiting the search to files of a certain type or age to improve performance. Using options like `-maxdepth` with `find` can limit the search depth, reducing the number of directories searched:

bash
Copy
```
find ~ -maxdepth 2 -name "*.txt"
```
Finally, **best practices** for searching files involve not just knowing which tools to use, but also understanding the context and your environment. In a multi-user system, always be mindful of the impact your searches may have on system performance. Avoid running intensive searches during peak usage times, as they can slow down the system for other users. Additionally, it's wise to avoid unnecessarily complex searches on production systems. For routine searches, consider running them during off-hours or using background job management tools like `nohup` to avoid interruptions.

In conclusion, becoming a pro at searching for files in Unix involves mastering a variety of tools and techniques. Whether you're using `find`, `grep`, `locate`, or even advanced tools like `fd` and `xargs`, each command has its own strengths and is designed to handle different scenarios. Combining these tools will allow you to tackle everything from simple file searches to complex, data-heavy tasks. Understanding how to refine and optimize your searches will save you time and make your Unix experience much more efficient.

So, the next time you find yourself hunting for a file or looking to extract specific data from a file, remember that with the right tools and techniques, searching in Unix is more like a treasure hunt than a chore. Use these tools to find exactly what you're looking for, and you'll be able to navigate your system with confidence, unlocking hidden gems of data in no time. Happy searching!

Chapter 13: Text Manipulation: Making Files Do the Twist

1. When it comes to working with text files on Unix, the real power lies not just in **reading** them, but in **manipulating** them. Whether you're transforming text, extracting specific columns from a CSV file, or even reformatting entire files, Unix offers a treasure trove of tools that let you twist, shape, and mold text with ease. In this chapter, we'll dive deep into the world of text manipulation. You'll learn how to perform common tasks like searching, replacing, and rearranging text, all while becoming more efficient with your workflow. Get ready to unleash the true power of Unix's text processing capabilities.

2. Let's start with one of the most essential tools for text manipulation: **cat**. The `cat` command is used to concatenate and display the contents of files. While it's often used to display the contents of a file to the terminal, it's also a great way to join multiple files together. For example, if you have two files—`file1.txt` and `file2.txt`—and you want to display their combined contents, simply run:
    bash
    Copy

```
cat file1.txt file2.txt
```

3.

    This command concatenates the two files and displays them in sequence. You can also use `cat` to create new files. By redirecting the output to a new file, you can create files with the combined contents:
    bash
    Copy

```
cat file1.txt file2.txt > combined.txt
```

4.

    `cat` is simple but powerful for manipulating text when you need to quickly join or display files.

5. Next up, let's talk about **grep**, a tool that's indispensable when it comes to searching for patterns in text. grep allows you to search for specific text within files, returning only the lines that match your search pattern. For instance, if you want to find all occurrences of the word "error" in a log file, you can use:
    bash
    Copy

    ```
    grep "error" logfile.txt
    ```

6.

    But grep isn't limited to just plain text. It also supports **regular expressions** (regex), which lets you search for more complex patterns. For example, if you want to find all lines that start with "error" (case-sensitive), you can use:
    bash
    Copy

    ```
    grep "^error" logfile.txt
    ```

7.

    The ^ symbol in regular expressions denotes the start of a line, making this search more specific. Whether you're searching for exact strings or using complex regular expressions, grep is your go-to command for finding text patterns within files.

8. Of course, searching isn't just about finding text—you'll often need to **replace** or **transform** it. Enter **sed** (stream editor). sed allows you to perform text transformations on files in a non-interactive manner, which is especially useful when working with large files or automating tasks. One of the most common uses for sed is search-and-replace. For example, to replace every occurrence of "apple" with "orange" in a file, you can run:
    bash
    Copy

    ```
    sed 's/apple/orange/g' file.txt
    ```

9.

The s stands for substitution, and the g tells sed to replace all occurrences in the file. This is a simple but powerful way to make bulk changes across many lines of text. If you want to make the change directly in the file, use the −i flag:

bash
Copy

```bash
sed -i 's/apple/orange/g' file.txt
```

10.

This replaces "apple" with "orange" in the file, modifying it in place. sed is one of the most powerful tools for text transformation in Unix, and its capabilities extend far beyond simple replacements.

11. Now that you're familiar with search and replace, let's explore how to **delete** text from files using sed. You can delete lines containing specific text with the d command. For example, to delete all lines containing the word "apple", you can use:

bash
Copy

```bash
sed '/apple/d' file.txt
```

12.

This will print the file with all lines containing "apple" removed. If you want to delete a range of lines, you can specify a range. For example, to delete lines 3 through 5, use:

bash
Copy

```bash
sed '3,5d' file.txt
```

13.

sed makes it easy to remove unwanted lines from files, whether they're based on a pattern or specific line numbers.

14. Sometimes, you might need to **insert** or **append** text into a file. With sed, you can do this as well. To insert a line of text before a specific line, use the i command. For example, to insert the text "Header: Report" before the second line of a file:

```bash
```
Copy

```
sed '2i Header: Report' file.txt
```

15.

Similarly, to append text after a specific line, use the `a` command:

```bash
```
Copy

```
sed '2a Footer: End of Report' file.txt
```
16.

These commands allow you to dynamically modify the content of a file by adding lines of text at specified locations.

17. While `sed` is great for modifying files line by line, **awk** is another powerful tool for text manipulation that operates on fields and columns within a file. `awk` is particularly useful for processing structured data, like CSV files or tab-delimited files. For example, to print the first column of a comma-separated file:

```bash
```
Copy

```
awk -F, '{print $1}' file.csv
```

18.

The `-F,` flag tells `awk` to use commas as the field delimiter, and `{print $1}` prints the first column. You can modify this to print any specific column, or even perform calculations on the data. For example, if the second column contains numbers, you can sum them up with:

```bash
```
Copy

```
awk -F, '{sum += $2} END {print sum}' file.csv
```
19.

awk gives you fine-grained control over your data, allowing you to split text into fields, perform calculations, and format the output.

20. Sometimes, you need to **rearrange** or **sort** text within a file. The `sort` command is perfect for this task. It sorts lines of text alphabetically, numerically, or according to other criteria. For example, to sort a list of names alphabetically, you can use:
bash
Copy

```
sort names.txt
```
21.

To sort numerically (for example, a list of numbers), use the `-n` option:
bash
Copy

```
sort -n numbers.txt
```
22.

You can also sort in reverse order with the `-r` flag:
bash
Copy

```
sort -r names.txt
```
23.

Sorting is a simple but powerful way to organize data, and `sort` is fast enough to handle large files with ease.

24. Another text manipulation task you might encounter is **splitting** or **joining** text. The `cut` command is perfect for extracting specific parts of a file. For example, if you have a file

with comma-separated values and you want to extract the second column, use:

bash
Copy

```
cut -d, -f2 file.csv
```

25.

The **-d** flag specifies the delimiter (in this case, a comma), and **-f2** tells `cut` to print the second field. You can also use `cut` to join text from multiple columns. For example, if you want to combine the first and second columns with a space between them, you can run:

bash
Copy

```
cut -d, -f1,2 file.csv | tr ',' ' '
```

26.

This command extracts the first and second columns and replaces the commas with spaces. The `tr` command is used to translate characters, and it's often used in combination with `cut` for more advanced text transformations.

27. Let's wrap things up by mentioning **tr**, the **translate** command, which is used for transforming or deleting characters. It's simple but incredibly powerful for quick transformations. For example, to convert all lowercase letters in a file to uppercase, you can use:

bash
Copy

```
tr 'a-z' 'A-Z' < input.txt > output.txt
```

28.

This command reads from `input.txt`, translates all lowercase letters to uppercase, and writes the result to `output.txt`. You can also use `tr` to delete characters or replace characters. For example, to remove all digits from a file:

bash

```
tr -d '0-9' < input.txt > output.txt
```
29.

30. In summary, Unix provides a wealth of tools for manipulating text, from simple commands like `cat` to powerful tools like `sed`, `awk`, and `grep`. Whether you're performing basic search-and-replace tasks, processing structured data, or reformatting text, Unix's text manipulation capabilities are incredibly flexible and powerful. By mastering these commands, you'll be able to automate complex tasks, process large datasets, and handle text files with confidence.

31. So, the next time you encounter a messy file, remember that with the right tools, you can make those files do the twist. Whether you're rearranging columns, removing unwanted characters, or replacing text, you now have the power to transform any file into exactly what you need. Take these techniques for a spin, and soon you'll be manipulating text like a Unix pro!

As you continue to work with text manipulation in Unix, it's worth remembering that **automation** is your best friend. Once you've mastered the basic commands like `sed`, `awk`, and `grep`, you'll start recognizing patterns in the text manipulation tasks you do regularly. This is the perfect time to begin writing **scripts** that can automate these processes, saving you valuable time and reducing the risk of errors.

For example, imagine you need to process a bunch of log files regularly. You could write a script that uses `grep` to find specific error messages, `sed` to clean up the data, and `awk` to summarize the results. By turning these steps into a script, you can execute all of them in one go without needing to manually input commands each time.

Here's a simple example of how you might automate the process of cleaning up log files:

bash
```bash
#!/bin/bash
# Process logs by finding "error" messages, cleaning up
data, and summarizing

# Find all error messages
grep "error" /var/log/*.log > errors.txt

# Remove timestamps (assuming timestamps are at the
beginning of each line)
```

```
sed -i 's/^[0-9]*-[0-9]*-[0-9]* //' errors.txt

# Count the number of error messages
awk '{print $1}' errors.txt | sort | uniq -c | sort -n >
error_summary.txt

echo "Error summary saved to error_summary.txt"
```

This script first searches for error messages in all `.log` files, cleans up the timestamps, and then counts and summarizes the errors. By saving this script as a file, such as `process_logs.sh`, you can run it every time you need to process logs with a single command. This is just one simple example, but once you get comfortable with scripting and text manipulation, the possibilities are endless.

Another powerful Unix tool for text manipulation is **sort**. As we mentioned earlier, **sort** can help you organize your data alphabetically or numerically, but it also allows for more complex operations like sorting by multiple columns. For example, let's say you have a file where each line consists of a name and a number, and you want to sort the data by the number, not the name. You can do that with **sort** like this:

bash
Copy
```
sort -k2,2n data.txt
```

The `-k2,2` option tells **sort** to sort by the second column, and the `n` flag specifies that the sort should be numeric (instead of lexicographic). This allows you to sort based on numbers rather than alphabetically. This is especially useful for dealing with datasets or logs where you need to sort based on specific fields.

A particularly handy technique in text manipulation is **using pipes** to chain commands together. In Unix, pipes (|) allow you to send the output of one command directly into the input of another. This is especially useful for combining text manipulation commands in a streamlined workflow. For example, if you want to find all occurrences of "error" in a file and then count how many times it appears, you can combine **grep** and **wc** (word count) like this:

bash
Copy
```
grep "error" file.txt | wc -l
```

This command uses **grep** to search for "error" and then passes the output (the lines containing "error") to **wc** `-l`, which counts the number of lines. Chaining commands like this is an incredibly efficient way to process data without having to manually intervene.

In some cases, you may want to manipulate text in a way that requires more **advanced scripting**. **Perl** and **Python** are both excellent tools for this. Both languages provide robust libraries for handling regular expressions, text manipulation, and even working with large files or datasets. Perl has long been a favorite for text processing, thanks to its powerful regular expression capabilities. Similarly, Python's `re` module and built-in file handling features make it an excellent choice for handling complex text manipulation tasks.

For example, let's say you need to search for a complex pattern in a large file and replace part of it using Python. Here's a simple Python script that does that:

python
Copy
```python
import re

with open('input.txt', 'r') as file:
    content = file.read()

# Replace occurrences of "apple" with "orange"
content = re.sub(r'apple', 'orange', content)

with open('output.txt', 'w') as file:
    file.write(content)
```
This Python script reads an input file, replaces "apple" with "orange," and writes the result to an output file. Using programming languages like Perl or Python can greatly extend your text manipulation capabilities, especially when working with more complex datasets or performing sophisticated tasks.

Another essential tool in text manipulation is **tee**. The `tee` command is useful when you want to **split** the output of a command so that you can send it to both a file and the screen. For example, if you're running a script and want to see the output while also saving it to a log file, you can use `tee`:

bash
Copy
```bash
some_command | tee output.log
```
This command will show the output on the screen and save it simultaneously to `output.log`. If you want to append to a file instead of overwriting it, use the `-a` option:

bash
Copy
```bash
some_command | tee -a output.log
```
`tee` is especially useful in debugging or logging scenarios where you need to capture the output of a long-running command while still being able to interact with it.

File encoding and character sets are often overlooked, but they are an important part of text manipulation. If you're working with text files that might contain special characters or different encodings, tools like **iconv** and **recode** can help you convert files between different character encodings. For instance, if you have a file in ISO-8859-1 encoding and need to convert it to UTF-8, you can use `iconv` like this:

```bash
iconv -f ISO-8859-1 -t UTF-8 input.txt > output.txt
```

This converts the file `input.txt` from ISO-8859-1 to UTF-8 and saves the result to `output.txt`. Converting text between different encodings is especially important when working with multilingual datasets or files that might have been generated on different platforms.

As you continue to work with text manipulation, keep in mind that the real power of Unix lies in its **composability**. Each tool is designed to do one thing well, and when you combine them, you can achieve incredibly powerful results. Whether you're using simple tools like `cat` and `grep` or advanced tools like `awk` and `sed`, Unix provides a flexible and efficient way to work with text.

In conclusion, text manipulation is one of the cornerstones of Unix. Whether you're transforming, analyzing, or reformatting text, the tools and techniques we've covered in this chapter will help you approach any text-related task with confidence. By mastering tools like `sed`, `awk`, `grep`, and `sort`, you'll be able to manipulate files with ease and create powerful automation scripts to handle repetitive tasks. The world of Unix text manipulation is vast, and the more you practice, the more creative you'll become with using these tools to make your files dance to your tune. So, get out there and start twisting text, because the power is now in your hands!

Chapter 14: The Power of Scripts: Making the Terminal Work for You

1. If you've ever found yourself performing the same set of commands over and over again, day in and day out, you may have wondered: "Isn't there a better way?" Well, wonder no more! In this chapter, we're diving into one of the most powerful aspects of Unix: **scripts**. Scripts are the secret sauce that turns simple terminal commands into powerful, automated workflows. With a few lines of code, you can transform repetitive tasks into streamlined, reusable operations, allowing the terminal to do all the hard work for you. Whether you're a developer, system administrator, or just someone who wants to speed up their workflow, writing scripts is a game changer. Get ready to unleash the full potential of your terminal with scripts that save you time, effort, and frustration.

2. **What is a script?** In Unix, a script is simply a file containing a series of commands that are executed in order. It's like a recipe for the terminal. Instead of typing individual commands over and over, you can write them all into a script and execute them in one go. Scripts can be used for a wide variety of tasks—automating backups, setting up environments, processing files, or even interacting with remote servers. The possibilities are endless. The best part? Once you write a script, you can run it any time you need it, and even modify it later to suit new needs. So let's roll up our sleeves and get started with the basics of writing and running your first script.

3. First things first: how do you create a script? A Unix script is simply a plain text file. You can create one with any text editor, whether it's `nano`, `vim`, or even a graphical editor like `gedit`. To begin, open your text editor and create a new file. Let's say you want to create a script that backs up a directory every time it's run. You can start by opening `nano` and typing:

bash
Copy

```
nano backup.sh
```

4.

This will open a new file called `backup.sh`. In this file, you'll write the commands that you want to execute automatically.

5. Now let's write your first script! At the top of every script, you need to define which **shell** the script will run with. This is called the **shebang** line. It tells the system which interpreter to use for running the script. For a basic shell script, you'll use:

bash
Copy

```
#!/bin/bash
```

6.

This tells the system to use the `bash` shell to interpret and execute the commands in the script. After this line, you can start adding the commands you want to automate. For instance, let's create a simple backup script that copies a directory to another location:

bash
Copy

```
#!/bin/bash
```

7. `# This script will back up the Documents folder to the backup directory`

8.

9. `cp -r ~/Documents ~/backup/`

10. `echo "Backup complete!"`

11.

The `cp -r` command copies the `Documents` directory (and all its contents) into the `backup` directory. The `echo` command prints "Backup complete!" to the terminal when the script finishes. Now you have a basic script that automates a backup task.

12. Once you've written your script, it's time to **make it executable**. By default, scripts aren't executable, meaning the system won't allow you to run them. To change this, use the `chmod` command to give your script execution permissions:
bash
Copy

```
chmod +x backup.sh
```

13.

This makes `backup.sh` executable. Now you can run your script by typing:
bash
Copy

```
./backup.sh
```

14.

This command tells the system to execute the script. If everything works correctly, it will perform the backup and display the "Backup complete!" message.

15. But wait—there's more! While simple scripts are great for automating tasks, **variables** allow you to make your scripts more flexible. A variable stores data that you can use throughout the script. For example, instead of hardcoding the backup directory, you could create a variable for it:
bash
Copy

```
#!/bin/bash
```

16. `# This script will back up a user-specified directory to the backup location`

17.

```
18.  BACKUP_DIR=~/Documents
19.  DEST_DIR=~/backup
20.
21.  cp -r $BACKUP_DIR $DEST_DIR
22.  echo "Backup of $BACKUP_DIR to $DEST_DIR complete!"
23.
```

Here, BACKUP_DIR and DEST_DIR are variables that store the source and destination paths. By using variables, you can easily modify the backup locations without changing the entire script.

24. **User input** is another powerful feature of scripts. Sometimes you'll want to get input from the person running the script, such as asking them to specify a directory or file. You can use the read command to capture user input. For example, let's modify the backup script to ask the user which directory they want to back up:

bash
Copy

```
#!/bin/bash

25.  # This script will back up a user-specified directory
26.
27.  echo "Enter the directory you want to back up:"
28.  read BACKUP_DIR
29.
30.  DEST_DIR=~/backup
31.
32.  cp -r $BACKUP_DIR $DEST_DIR
33.  echo "Backup of $BACKUP_DIR to $DEST_DIR complete!"
34.
```

Now, when you run the script, it will prompt the user to enter the directory they want to back up. This makes your script more interactive and adaptable to different situations.

35. You can also use **conditional statements** to make your scripts smarter. For example, you might want to check if the directory the user entered exists before proceeding with the backup. In this case, you can use an if statement:

bash
Copy

```
#!/bin/bash
```

36. # This script will back up a user-specified directory
    if it exists
37.
38. echo "Enter the directory you want to back up:"
39. read BACKUP_DIR
40.
41. DEST_DIR=~/backup
42.
43. if [-d "$BACKUP_DIR"]; then
44.   cp -r $BACKUP_DIR $DEST_DIR
45.   echo "Backup of $BACKUP_DIR to $DEST_DIR complete!"
46. else
47.   echo "Error: $BACKUP_DIR does not exist."
48. fi
49.

The if [-d "$BACKUP_DIR"] statement checks if the directory exists. If it does, the script performs the backup; otherwise, it prints an error message. Conditional statements give your scripts the ability to make decisions based on user input, system status, or other conditions.

50. **Loops** are another essential feature of scripting. A loop allows you to execute a set of commands repeatedly. For instance, if you want to back up multiple directories at once, you can create a **for** loop:

bash
Copy

```
#!/bin/bash
```

51. # This script will back up multiple directories
52.
53. BACKUP_DIRS=("~/Documents" "~/Pictures" "~/Videos")
54. DEST_DIR=~/backup
55.
56. for DIR in "${BACKUP_DIRS[@]}"; do
57.   cp -r $DIR $DEST_DIR
58.   echo "Backup of $DIR to $DEST_DIR complete!"
```
```

59. `done`
60.

Here, the `for` loop iterates over each directory in the `BACKUP_DIRS` array and performs the backup for each one. Loops are powerful because they let you repeat tasks without having to write the same code over and over.

61. **Error handling** is an essential part of any script, especially if it's doing something critical like backing up files. You want to ensure that if something goes wrong, the script handles it gracefully. You can use `exit` codes to detect errors and take action accordingly. For example:

`bash`

Copy

```bash
#!/bin/bash
```

62. `# This script backs up a directory and checks for errors`
63.
64. `BACKUP_DIR=~/Documents`
65. `DEST_DIR=~/backup`
66.
67. `if [ ! -d "$BACKUP_DIR" ]; then`
68. `    echo "Error: $BACKUP_DIR does not exist."`
69. `    exit 1`
70. `fi`
71.
72. `cp -r $BACKUP_DIR $DEST_DIR`
73. `if [ $? -eq 0 ]; then`
74. `    echo "Backup complete!"`
75. `else`
76. `    echo "Error: Backup failed."`
77. `    exit 1`
78. `fi`
79.

In this example, if the source directory doesn't exist, the script exits with an error message. The `cp` command also checks the exit status (`$?`), ensuring that the backup succeeded before reporting success. Error handling ensures that your scripts behave predictably, even in unexpected situations.

80. **Scheduling scripts** is a great way to automate tasks without needing to manually run the script each time. Unix's `cron` service lets you schedule tasks to run at specific times or intervals. For example, to schedule your backup script to run every day at 2 AM, you can use `crontab`:

bash
Copy

```
crontab -e
```

81.

This will open the crontab file for editing. You can add a line like:

bash
Copy

```
0 2 * * * /path/to/backup.sh
```

82.

This line tells `cron` to run your backup script every day at 2 AM. Cron jobs are an incredibly efficient way to automate routine tasks without manual intervention.

83. In conclusion, writing scripts is one of the most powerful ways to extend the functionality of the Unix terminal. Whether you're automating backups, processing files, or scheduling regular tasks, scripting makes your life easier and your workflow more efficient. From basic commands and variables to advanced concepts like loops and error handling, mastering scripts will give you full control over your system and its tasks. So go ahead, start writing scripts that make the terminal work for you, and turn your repetitive tasks into a breeze!

As you become more comfortable with writing and automating scripts, you'll begin to notice the power of **modularity**. Instead of writing large, monolithic scripts that try to do everything at once, break your tasks down into smaller, reusable functions. Functions allow you to write blocks of code that perform specific tasks, which can then be reused throughout your script. This makes your scripts more organized, easier to maintain, and less prone to errors.

Here's an example of how you might use functions in a backup script:

bash
Copy

```bash
#!/bin/bash
# This script uses functions to back up directories

BACKUP_DIR=~/Documents
DEST_DIR=~/backup

# Function to check if the directory exists
check_directory() {
    if [ ! -d "$1" ]; then
        echo "Error: $1 does not exist."
        exit 1
    fi
}

# Function to perform the backup
perform_backup() {
    cp -r $1 $2
    echo "Backup of $1 to $2 complete!"
}

# Use the functions
check_directory $BACKUP_DIR
perform_backup $BACKUP_DIR $DEST_DIR
```

By breaking the script into `check_directory` and `perform_backup` functions, it's easier to understand and maintain. You can now reuse these functions for different tasks or even in other scripts. Modularity helps keep your code clean and efficient, allowing you to focus on logic instead of repeating code.

Debugging is an inevitable part of scripting, especially as scripts grow more complex. Thankfully, Unix provides several tools to help you find and fix errors. The `set -x` command enables **debugging mode**, which prints each command as it's executed, allowing you to track down issues step-by-step. For example:

```
bash
```
Copy
```bash
#!/bin/bash
set -x  # Enable debugging

BACKUP_DIR=~/Documents
DEST_DIR=~/backup
```

```
cp -r $BACKUP_DIR $DEST_DIR
echo "Backup complete!"
```
When you run this script, it will print every command and its arguments to the terminal as it's executed. This can be extremely helpful when troubleshooting issues, as you'll see exactly where the script is going wrong.

Similarly, you can use `set -e` to stop the script as soon as any command fails, which helps to catch errors early in execution. For instance:

bash
Copy
```
set -e  # Exit on first error
```
This combination of `set -x` and `set -e` gives you powerful tools for debugging and troubleshooting your scripts, allowing you to pinpoint errors and fix them quickly.

As you become a more advanced user of Unix, you'll likely encounter situations where you need to handle **file permissions** within your scripts. For example, you may need to ensure that a script has the proper permissions to read, write, or execute certain files. You can manage permissions with the `chmod`, `chown`, and `chgrp` commands directly in your script.

For instance, if you want to ensure that the backup directory has the correct write permissions before running your backup script, you can add this to your script:

bash
Copy
```
#!/bin/bash
# Ensure correct permissions before backing up

chmod u+rwx ~/backup
```
This command grants read, write, and execute permissions to the user for the backup directory. Similarly, you can change the ownership of files or directories using `chown`, or modify group permissions with `chgrp`. Incorporating these commands into your scripts ensures that all necessary files are accessible to your script, regardless of their current permissions.

As your scripts grow in complexity, **logging** becomes an essential practice. Logging lets you track what your script is doing, what errors occur, and when specific tasks are completed. You can easily add logging to your script using the `echo` command or redirecting output to a file.

For example, you might want to log the start and end times of your backup script:

bash
Copy
```
#!/bin/bash
LOGFILE="backup.log"
```

```
echo "Backup started at $(date)" >> $LOGFILE

cp -r ~/Documents ~/backup/
echo "Backup completed at $(date)" >> $LOGFILE
```
This simple logging approach appends the date and time to a log file, making it easy to track the script's execution. For more advanced logging, you can include different log levels (e.g., info, warning, error) or use a logging framework. With logging, you'll have a clear record of what happens each time your script runs.

As you dive deeper into Unix scripting, you'll also want to explore **advanced automation tools** like `cron` and `at` for scheduling scripts. While we briefly touched on `cron` for running scripts at scheduled times, `at` is another useful tool that allows you to schedule a script to run once at a specific time in the future. For instance:

bash
Copy
```
echo "/path/to/script.sh" | at 3:00 PM
```
This schedules the `script.sh` to run at 3:00 PM today. `cron` is excellent for recurring tasks, while `at` is perfect for one-time scheduled tasks. Mastering both will significantly expand the power of your scripts.

Another useful tool for automating your workflow is **alias**, which allows you to create custom commands or shortcuts for frequently used scripts. Instead of typing out long script names or commands, you can define an alias in your shell's configuration file (`~/.bashrc` or `~/.bash_profile`) to simplify the process.

For example, if you regularly back up your `Documents` folder, you can create an alias for your backup script:

bash
Copy
```
alias backupdocs="bash ~/scripts/backup.sh"
```
Now, every time you type `backupdocs` in the terminal, it will run your `backup.sh` script. This saves you from having to remember long file paths or script names, streamlining your workflow even further.

Version control is another essential practice when it comes to managing your scripts. As your scripts grow more complex, it becomes increasingly important to track changes and maintain a history of revisions. Tools like **Git** allow you to version-control your scripts, making it easy to roll back to previous versions, collaborate with others, and keep track of improvements or bug fixes.

For example, after creating a script, you can initialize a Git repository in the script's directory:

```bash
Copy
git init
git add backup.sh
git commit -m "Initial commit of backup script"
```
By using version control, you ensure that your scripts are well-managed and that you have a history of changes, which can be helpful when troubleshooting or collaborating.

In conclusion, scripting is one of the most powerful ways to **automate** your tasks in Unix. From basic backups to complex workflows, writing scripts allows you to save time, reduce errors, and improve efficiency. By mastering scripting techniques like variables, loops, conditionals, error handling, and scheduling, you can take full control of your Unix environment and create a seamless, automated workflow. The terminal will no longer be something you just type into—it'll become your own personal assistant, ready to handle any task you throw at it. So start writing scripts, automate your processes, and let the terminal work for you!

Chapter 15: The Art of File Compression: Zip, Unzip, and Win

1. In the world of computers, files grow bigger by the day. Whether it's images, documents, or entire projects, the amount of data we store can quickly become unwieldy. Fortunately, there's a solution: **compression**. Compressing files allows us to reduce their size, making storage and transfer faster and more efficient. In this chapter, we're going to delve into the art of file compression on Unix systems. You'll learn how to zip and unzip files, compress multiple files into archives, and explore different compression formats, so you can handle your files with the utmost efficiency.

2. **Why compress files?** Compressing files has many benefits, including:

   o **Saving disk space**: Compressed files take up less space, which is especially useful on systems with limited storage.

   o **Faster transfers**: Smaller files are quicker to upload, download, or send over email.

   o **Organizing multiple files**: Compressing files into a single archive makes it easier to handle and move around many files at once.

3. But how do you go about compressing and decompressing files? Let's explore the basic tools you'll need to start using compression effectively.

4. The most widely used compression utility on Unix systems is **gzip** (short for GNU zip). `gzip` is a simple command-line tool that compresses files to a `.gz` format. To compress a file, simply run the following command:

```bash
Copy
```

```
gzip filename.txt
```

5.

This will create a compressed file called `filename.txt.gz` and delete the original file (`filename.txt`) by default. If you want to keep the original file and just create the compressed version, use the `-k` flag:

bash
Copy

```
gzip -k filename.txt
```

6.

The `-k` flag tells `gzip` to keep the original file while also creating the compressed `.gz` file.

7. To **decompress** a `.gz` file, you can use the `gunzip` command:

bash
Copy

```
gunzip filename.txt.gz
```

8.

This will decompress the file and return it to its original state. You can also use the `-k` flag with `gunzip` if you want to keep the `.gz` file:

bash
Copy

```
gunzip -k filename.txt.gz
```

9.

This allows you to retain both the original compressed file and the decompressed version.

10. If you need to compress or decompress multiple files at once, you can use `gzip` with wildcards. For example, to compress all `.txt` files in the current directory, you can run:

bash
Copy

```
gzip *.txt
```

11.

This will compress every `.txt` file in the directory, creating `.gz` files for each. Similarly, you can decompress multiple `.gz` files at once by running:

bash
Copy

```
gunzip *.gz
```

12.

13. While `gzip` is great for single files, what if you want to compress a whole bunch of files into one **archive**? Enter **tar**, the Unix utility for creating archive files. `tar` stands for **tape archive**, and it's commonly used to package multiple files or directories into a single archive file. The great thing about `tar` is that it doesn't just compress files—it also allows you to bundle them together in a single file for easy storage or transfer.

To create a basic archive, you can use the `-c` (create) and `-f` (file) options, like this:

bash
Copy

```
tar -cf archive.tar file1.txt file2.txt
```

14.

This command will create an archive called `archive.tar` containing `file1.txt` and `file2.txt`. Note that `tar` doesn't compress the files by default—it just bundles them into a single archive. But you can easily add compression by using the `-z` option, which tells `tar` to use `gzip` compression:

bash

```
tar -czf archive.tar.gz file1.txt file2.txt
```

15.

This will create a compressed archive (`.tar.gz`) that contains the two files.

16. To **extract** the contents of a `.tar.gz` archive, you can use the `-x` (extract) option along with `-f`:

bash

```
tar -xzf archive.tar.gz
```

17.

This will decompress and extract the files from `archive.tar.gz` into the current directory. You can also specify a directory to extract the files to:

bash

```
tar -xzf archive.tar.gz -C /path/to/directory
```

18.

19. While `.tar.gz` is a commonly used compression format, there are other formats you might encounter, such as **`.tar.bz2`** (created using `bzip2`) or **`.tar.xz`** (created using `xz`). These formats use different compression algorithms that can offer better compression ratios or faster speeds. To create a `.tar.bz2` archive, use:

bash

```
tar -cjf archive.tar.bz2 file1.txt file2.txt
```

20.

And to extract it:

bash
Copy

```
tar -xjf archive.tar.bz2
```

21.

Similarly, to create a `.tar.xz` archive, you can run:

bash
Copy

```
tar -caf archive.tar.xz file1.txt file2.txt
```

22.

And to extract it:

bash
Copy

```
tar -xaf archive.tar.xz
```

23.

24. **zip** and **unzip** are other popular compression utilities, especially for those working with cross-platform systems or needing `.zip` archives. `zip` is used to create `.zip` archives, and `unzip` is used to extract them. To create a `.zip` file containing `file1.txt` and `file2.txt`, use:

bash
Copy

```
zip archive.zip file1.txt file2.txt
```

25.

This will create the archive `archive.zip` containing both files. To extract the contents of a `.zip` file, use:

bash
Copy

```
unzip archive.zip
```

26.

27. One of the most useful features of `zip` is the ability to compress files and directories recursively. You can add the `-r` flag to `zip` to compress an entire directory, including all its subdirectories:

bash
Copy

```
zip -r archive.zip directory_name/
```

28.

This will compress `directory_name` and everything inside it into a `.zip` archive. This is especially useful for packaging up large directories for storage or transfer.

29. **Compression ratio** is an important consideration when choosing your compression method. While `gzip` is generally faster, its compression ratio (how much it reduces the size of the file) might not be the best. On the other hand, `bzip2` and `xz` typically achieve better compression ratios but take longer to compress. If speed is your priority, go with `gzip`. If you're dealing with very large files and want the best compression possible, use `bzip2` or `xz`.

30. Another important concept to grasp is **password protection** when compressing files. If you want to secure your archive with a password to prevent unauthorized access, `zip` has an option for that. Use the `-e` flag to encrypt a `.zip` file:

bash
Copy

```
zip -e archive.zip file1.txt
```

31.

This will prompt you to enter a password to protect the archive. When someone tries to extract it, they'll need the password. This is a simple way to add an extra layer of security to your compressed files.

32. **Managing large archives** often requires more than just compression. You might need to **split** an archive into smaller parts to make it easier to transfer over the network or store on a medium with limited space. With `split` and `cat`, you can break a large file into smaller chunks and later reassemble it. For example, to split a large file into smaller pieces, you can use:

bash
Copy

```
split -b 100M largefile.tar.gz part_
```

33.

This will break `largefile.tar.gz` into 100MB chunks, with each part being named `part_aa`, `part_ab`, and so on. To reassemble the parts, you can use `cat`:

bash
Copy

```
cat part_* > largefile.tar.gz
```

34.

35. **Disk space** is another area where compression shines. If you're running low on space but don't want to delete files, consider compressing them into archives. This can free up a significant amount of space while preserving your files. Just keep in mind that compressing files with highly compressed formats like `.tar.gz` or `.zip` may require some processing power to decompress later.

36. **In conclusion**, file compression is one of the most useful tools in Unix for saving space, organizing files, and speeding up transfers. Whether you're using `gzip`, `tar`, `zip`, or other compression tools, understanding how and when to use each format will allow you to manage files more efficiently. By incorporating compression into your workflow, you'll be able to store and share files faster, keep your system organized, and handle large datasets with ease. So the next time you're working with a huge batch of files, remember that compression is your ally—whether you need speed, space, or security. Happy compressing!

Compression and Backup are an essential part of managing data in Unix, especially for system administrators and power users. One common use case for compression is during **backup** processes. When backing up large directories, you can create a compressed archive to save space and facilitate quicker transfers. For example, when you perform a system backup or backup of important directories, you might want to compress it so it doesn't take up too much disk space. Here's how you can use `tar` with compression:

```bash
Copy
tar -czf backup.tar.gz /home/user
```

This command creates a compressed archive of the `/home/user` directory, making it easier to store or transfer. This is particularly helpful if you need to backup multiple directories or large datasets and need to reduce the total size of the backup for better efficiency.

Compressed file formats and compatibility are another consideration when choosing a compression method. Different tools create different types of compressed files. For instance, `.gz` files created by `gzip` are very commonly used in Linux and Unix systems, but other systems (like Windows) may not handle them as easily. Similarly, `.zip` files are often used for compatibility with Windows systems. If you need to ensure that your compressed files can be opened across different platforms, consider using `.zip` or `.tar.gz`, which are supported by a wide variety of operating systems. Understanding which formats are compatible with your environment will help you choose the right tool for the job.

Working with large archives can be a bit tricky, especially if you need to extract parts of an archive without decompressing the entire file. For instance, `tar` has options for listing the contents of an archive without extracting it. To view the contents of a `.tar.gz` archive, use the `-t` option:

```bash
Copy
tar -tzf archive.tar.gz
```

This will display a list of files within the archive, allowing you to check its contents before extracting it. Similarly, if you only want to extract specific files from an archive, you can do so by specifying the file paths:

```bash
Copy
tar -xzf archive.tar.gz specificfile.txt
```

This command extracts only `specificfile.txt` from the archive, saving you time and space when working with large archives.

File integrity and checksums are often important when transferring compressed files, especially if you're moving files across a network or to external storage devices. To ensure that the file has not been corrupted during the transfer, you can use tools like `md5sum` or `sha256sum` to generate and verify checksums.

To generate an MD5 checksum for a compressed file, you can run:

```bash
md5sum archive.tar.gz
```

This will return a checksum value, which you can store and verify after transferring the file to ensure its integrity. When you receive the file back, you can check its checksum by running `md5sum` again on the new file. If the values match, you can be sure that the file was transferred successfully and hasn't been corrupted.

Compression for cloud storage is also a critical consideration when storing large files or backups in the cloud. Many cloud storage providers, such as Google Drive, Dropbox, or AWS S3, offer large storage limits but may have performance or bandwidth limitations. Compressing files before uploading them can help with both storage efficiency and upload/download speed. By compressing files, you minimize the amount of data transferred, which can result in faster uploads and lower bandwidth consumption.

Another important aspect of file compression is **archiving for software distribution**. Developers often use compression tools to package and distribute software, libraries, and documentation. For example, when you download source code from repositories or install software packages, it's often compressed in `.tar.gz`, `.tar.bz2`, or `.zip` format. Compression helps minimize download sizes, especially for larger software packages, making distribution more efficient.

Best practices for compression include:

- **Choose the right format**: Use `.tar.gz` or `.zip` for compatibility across different platforms. Use `.tar.xz` or `.tar.bz2` if you need better compression ratios.

- **Compress regularly**: Regularly compress files that aren't accessed often, like old logs or backups, to save space.

- **Use password protection**: For sensitive data, always password-protect compressed files (e.g., with `zip -e` or `gpg` encryption).

- **Test and verify**: Always test your compressed files by extracting them in a separate location to ensure they are intact and accessible.

- **Split large archives**: If dealing with very large files, consider splitting them into smaller parts to make them easier to transfer or store.

In conclusion, file compression is an essential skill for efficiently managing files in Unix. From compressing individual files to creating multi-file archives, Unix provides a wide range of tools for reducing file sizes and organizing data. Whether you're working with backups, software distribution, or simply trying to save space, mastering compression utilities like `gzip`, `tar`, `zip`, and `bzip2` will make you more efficient and productive in handling your files. With the techniques you've learned in this chapter, you'll be able to handle compression like a pro, whether it's for day-to-day tasks or large-scale data management. Compress, archive, and transfer with confidence—Unix has you covered!

Chapter 16: Networking Basics: Unix and the Internet's Secret Life

1. At the heart of modern computing is **networking**—the invisible thread that connects everything, from your local machine to servers halfway across the world. Whether you're browsing the web, sending emails, or downloading files, networking is the foundation that makes it all happen. In this chapter, we'll uncover the **secret life** of Unix networking, showing you how Unix systems connect to and communicate over the internet. By understanding networking basics, you'll be able to manage connections, troubleshoot issues, and make the most of your Unix system's ability to interact with other machines, whether locally or globally. Let's dive into the nuts and bolts of networking and uncover how Unix makes it all work.

2. **What is networking?** In the simplest terms, networking is the process of connecting computers to share resources, data, or services. It allows systems to communicate with each other over both local and wide-area networks (LANs and WANs), forming the backbone of everything from a home network to the entire internet. In Unix, networking is managed through a collection of commands and tools that allow you to view, configure, and troubleshoot network connections. Unix is known for its powerful networking tools, which give you fine-grained control over your system's interactions with other devices.

3. To get started, let's discuss **IP addresses**—the unique identifiers assigned to devices on a network. Just as your home address allows the postal service to deliver mail, an IP address lets networked systems find each other. An IP address can either be **IPv4** (e.g., 192.168.0.1) or **IPv6** (e.g., 2001:0db8:85a3:0000:0000:8a2e:0370:7334). Most modern systems, including Unix-based ones, are configured to use **DHCP** (Dynamic Host Configuration Protocol), which automatically assigns an IP address to your device when it connects to the network.

4. To view the IP address of your Unix machine, the `ifconfig` command (or `ip` on some distributions) is your first stop. Running `ifconfig` will display the network interfaces on your system and their associated IP addresses:

bash
Copy

```
ifconfig
```

5.

In this output, you'll see a list of network interfaces such as `eth0`, `wlan0`, or `lo` (for loopback), along with their assigned IP addresses. For a more modern approach to viewing network configuration, use the `ip` command:

bash
Copy

```
ip addr show
```

6.

This command will provide detailed information about all active network interfaces and their IP addresses.

7. Once you know your machine's IP address, you'll need to understand **network interfaces**. A network interface is simply the point of connection between your computer and the network. In Unix, interfaces can be physical (like an Ethernet card or Wi-Fi adapter) or virtual (such as loopback interfaces used for internal communication). The loopback interface, `lo`, has the special IP address `127.0.0.1`, which always points back to your local machine.

8. **DNS (Domain Name System)** is another critical concept in networking. DNS acts as the "phone book" of the internet, translating human-readable domain names (like `www.google.com`) into machine-readable IP addresses. Without DNS, you'd need to remember the numerical IP address of every website you visit! To check your DNS configuration on Unix, you can view the `/etc/resolv.conf` file, which contains the addresses of DNS servers:

bash
Copy

```
cat /etc/resolv.conf
```

9.

This file lists the nameservers your system uses to resolve domain names. If you want to change your DNS servers (for example, to use Google's DNS at `8.8.8.8`), you can modify this file, but keep in mind that some systems may manage this configuration through network management tools.

10. Now that you understand IP addresses and DNS, let's look at how Unix connects to other systems using **network protocols**. The two most common networking protocols are **TCP (Transmission Control Protocol)** and **UDP (User Datagram Protocol)**. TCP is reliable,

ensuring that data is delivered correctly and in order, making it ideal for applications like web browsing and file transfers. UDP, on the other hand, is faster but less reliable, making it suitable for streaming and real-time communications.

11. When your system communicates over a network, it uses **ports** to identify specific services. For instance, web servers use **port 80** for HTTP and **port 443** for HTTPS. Each service running on your machine listens for incoming connections on a specific port. To see which services are listening on which ports, you can use the `netstat` command:
bash
Copy

```
netstat -tuln
```

12.

This will display a list of open ports and the services associated with them. The `-t` flag shows TCP connections, the `-u` flag shows UDP connections, and `-l` shows listening ports. If you're troubleshooting a service or ensuring that your system is properly configured, this command is invaluable.

13. **Ping** is one of the most basic networking commands, used to test the reachability of a host on the network. If you want to check if a particular machine is reachable, you can use the `ping` command followed by the target's IP address or domain name:
bash
Copy

```
ping 8.8.8.8
```

14.

This sends ICMP echo requests to `8.8.8.8` (Google's public DNS) and waits for a response. If the machine is reachable, you'll see replies with the round-trip time in milliseconds. If not, you'll receive an error indicating that the host is unreachable. `ping` is a quick and simple way to check connectivity to remote systems.

15. Another useful tool for troubleshooting network connections is **Traceroute**, which shows the path that packets take from your machine to a remote host. Traceroute helps identify where delays or failures occur in the network. To run `traceroute`, simply type:
bash
Copy

```
traceroute www.google.com
```

16.

This will display each hop along the way, starting from your machine to the target. You can identify bottlenecks or problematic network segments that are causing slowdowns or dropped connections.

17. **SSH (Secure Shell)** is a protocol used for securely accessing remote systems over a network. With SSH, you can remotely log into a machine, execute commands, and transfer files as if you were sitting right in front of it. To connect to a remote machine, you simply use the `ssh` command followed by the username and IP address of the remote machine:

bash
Copy

```
ssh user@192.168.0.100
```

18.

This will prompt you for the remote machine's password, and once authenticated, you'll have access to the remote system's terminal. SSH is an essential tool for system administrators and anyone who needs to manage remote servers.

19. For transferring files securely between machines, **SCP (Secure Copy Protocol)** is an excellent tool. `scp` uses SSH to copy files between local and remote systems. For example, to copy a file from your local machine to a remote machine, you can run:

bash
Copy

```
scp file.txt user@192.168.0.100:/remote/directory
```

20.

This will copy `file.txt` to the specified directory on the remote machine. You can also use `scp` to copy files in the opposite direction, from the remote machine to your local system.

21. **Firewall management** is another important aspect of Unix networking. Firewalls control incoming and outgoing network traffic, allowing you to specify which services and ports

are accessible. On Unix systems, you can manage firewall settings with **iptables** or **firewalld** (depending on your distribution). To list the current iptables rules, you can run:
bash
Copy

```
sudo iptables -L
```

22.

To add a rule that allows incoming HTTP traffic (port 80), use:
bash
Copy

```
sudo iptables -A INPUT -p tcp --dport 80 -j ACCEPT
```
23.

Firewalls are crucial for securing your system, and it's important to configure them properly to prevent unauthorized access while still allowing necessary traffic.

24. **Network troubleshooting** tools like `nslookup` and **dig** are invaluable when diagnosing DNS-related issues. `nslookup` allows you to query DNS records for a domain:
bash
Copy

```
nslookup www.google.com
```

25.

This will return the IP address associated with `www.google.com`. Similarly, `dig` provides detailed DNS query information:
bash
Copy

```
dig www.google.com
```

Both of these tools are essential when diagnosing DNS resolution issues and ensuring that your system is correctly resolving domain names.

27. In conclusion, networking is the backbone of modern computing, and Unix provides a rich set of tools to connect, configure, and troubleshoot your system's network connections. From checking IP addresses and managing network interfaces to troubleshooting connectivity with tools like `ping` and `traceroute`, Unix gives you the power to understand and control your network interactions. Whether you're managing a server, connecting to remote machines via SSH, or ensuring that your system is securely accessible, mastering these networking basics will give you the skills needed to keep your systems connected and running smoothly. So go ahead—explore the secret life of Unix networking and start making the most of your system's internet capabilities!

Network Security is a crucial aspect of any network, especially when you're working with Unix systems. Ensuring your system is secure from malicious attacks or unauthorized access should be one of your top priorities. A good starting point for securing your network is by configuring the **SSH** service properly. For example, disabling password-based authentication and enforcing the use of SSH keys for authentication can significantly improve the security of your remote connections.

To disable password-based authentication and force SSH key-based login, you can edit the SSH configuration file `/etc/ssh/sshd_config`:

```bash
Copy
sudo nano /etc/ssh/sshd_config
```

Look for the line `PasswordAuthentication` and set it to `no`:

```bash
Copy
PasswordAuthentication no
```

This forces SSH to use only key-based authentication, significantly increasing the security of your connections. After making changes, restart the SSH service:

```bash
Copy
sudo systemctl restart sshd
```

VPNs (Virtual Private Networks) are another important tool for securing network connections. If you're accessing a remote network or working from an untrusted environment, a VPN can encrypt your traffic and provide a secure tunnel for data transmission. Many Unix systems support VPNs, and there are various protocols like **OpenVPN**, **IPsec**, and **WireGuard** you can use to create secure connections. Installing and configuring a VPN client on your Unix system is relatively straightforward, and it ensures that your data is safe from eavesdropping while traveling across untrusted networks like public Wi-Fi.

One critical aspect of network security is ensuring your machine is not running unnecessary **open ports** or services. Each open port on your system is a potential point of attack, and keeping only the necessary services running reduces your exposure to vulnerabilities. To check which ports are open and which services are listening, you can use the **ss** command:

bash
Copy
```
ss -tuln
```
This will list all open TCP and UDP ports, along with the corresponding services. By reviewing this list regularly, you can identify and close unused ports, improving the security of your system.

Updating your system regularly is another essential security measure. Many Unix-based systems, especially those running Linux, have package managers that make it easy to apply security patches and updates. For example, on a Debian-based system like Ubuntu, you can run the following commands to update your system:

bash
Copy
```
sudo apt update
sudo apt upgrade
```
Keeping your system and its packages up to date ensures that you're protected against known vulnerabilities. Always stay on top of updates, as new exploits are discovered regularly.

Network Monitoring tools are also a key part of keeping your system secure and running smoothly. Tools like **netstat**, **iftop**, and **nmap** allow you to monitor network traffic, identify suspicious activity, and diagnose network issues. For example, **iftop** provides real-time statistics on network usage, showing which processes are consuming bandwidth:

bash
Copy
```
sudo iftop
```
You can also use **nmap** to scan your system for open ports and potential security weaknesses. Running a simple **nmap** scan to identify open ports on your system looks like this:

bash
Copy
```
sudo nmap -sT localhost
```
Regular network monitoring can help you catch security issues early, before they become critical.

Bandwidth and Traffic Control are often overlooked but essential in managing network performance. Whether you're running a server or just using a personal machine, it's important to monitor your network traffic and ensure that you're not overloading your network connection. Tools like **tc** (Traffic Control) and **iptables** allow you to set up traffic shaping and bandwidth limits, so you can prioritize critical services or limit unnecessary traffic. For example, if you want to limit a particular service to only use a certain amount of bandwidth, tc can help you set that up.

Troubleshooting Networking Issues is a part of any network administrator's life. Whether it's slow connections, intermittent access, or completely no connectivity, diagnosing network issues requires a systematic approach. Besides the ping and traceroute tools, **netcat** (also called nc) is a useful tool for testing connectivity between two machines. You can use it to check if a particular port is open on a remote machine:

On the remote server:

```bash
nc -l 12345
```
On the client machine:

```bash
nc <remote-server-ip> 12345
```
This establishes a simple connection to the server on port 12345, allowing you to test if the port is open and the connection is functional. netcat is an excellent diagnostic tool for checking basic connectivity and port status.

As you manage more advanced networks, you may find yourself dealing with **routing**. Understanding basic routing concepts and tools like **ip route** will allow you to manage network traffic more effectively. For instance, you can view your routing table with:

```bash
ip route
```
This will show you how network packets are routed between different networks. If you're working with multiple interfaces or virtual networks, understanding routing will be critical to ensuring traffic flows correctly between systems.

Firewalls are perhaps one of the most important tools in network security. They protect your system from unauthorized access and ensure that only trusted traffic can enter or exit your system. On many Unix systems, iptables or firewalld are used to configure and manage firewalls. You can use iptables to create rules that allow or deny traffic based on IP addresses, ports, and protocols.

For example, to block incoming SSH connections from a specific IP address, you can run:

```bash
Copy
sudo iptables -A INPUT -p tcp --dport 22 -s <blocked-ip> -j DROP
```

This command adds a rule to block incoming SSH connections from the specified IP address. Proper firewall configuration is a critical step in securing your Unix system.

In conclusion, understanding the basics of networking is crucial for anyone using or managing a Unix-based system. From checking your IP address and managing DNS settings to troubleshooting connectivity issues and securing your network, mastering networking commands and concepts will empower you to fully control your system's connections to the wider world. By using tools like `ping`, `netstat`, `traceroute`, and `ssh`, along with best practices for security and monitoring, you can ensure that your system remains connected, secure, and efficient. Networking is the lifeblood of modern computing, and with Unix's robust networking tools at your disposal, you'll be well-equipped to navigate the digital landscape with confidence. So, explore, configure, and monitor your networks like a pro!

Chapter 17: Managing Software: Because Sometimes, Things Need Updates

1. One of the most important aspects of maintaining any Unix system is **managing software**—whether that means installing new software, updating existing packages, or removing outdated ones. In the fast-paced world of software development, updates aren't just about getting new features; they often include important security patches, bug fixes, and performance improvements. Keeping your system's software up to date is essential for ensuring that everything runs smoothly, securely, and efficiently. In this chapter, we'll dive into the art of managing software on Unix systems. Whether you're using package managers, compiling from source, or configuring repositories, we've got you covered. Let's take a look at the best ways to keep your system in tip-top shape.

2. **Package Managers** are your best friend when it comes to managing software on Unix systems. These tools automate the process of installing, updating, and removing software packages. Most Linux distributions use a package manager, which simplifies the task of keeping your system up to date. There are different package managers depending on the distribution you're using. Some of the most common ones are:

   o **APT** (Advanced Package Tool) for Debian-based systems (like Ubuntu)

   o **YUM** (Yellowdog Updater, Modified) for Red Hat-based systems (like Fedora or CentOS)

   o **Pacman** for Arch Linux

   o **Zypper** for SUSE-based systems

3. These package managers connect to online repositories, where they download and install software packages. They can also handle dependencies automatically, ensuring that any required libraries or tools are installed alongside the main software package.

4. **Installing Software** with a package manager is typically straightforward. For example, to install a new program using **APT** on Ubuntu or Debian, you can run:
bash
Copy

```
sudo apt update
```
5. `sudo apt install <package-name>`
6.

The `apt update` command updates the list of available packages from the repositories, and `apt install` installs the specified package. For example, if you wanted to install the popular text editor `vim`, you'd run:
bash
Copy

```
sudo apt install vim
```
7.

On Red Hat-based systems using **YUM**, you'd run:
bash
Copy

```
sudo yum install vim
```
8.

Package managers make installing software quick and easy. They take care of finding the correct versions and resolving dependencies, saving you the hassle of manually downloading and configuring software.

9. **Updating Software** is one of the most important tasks in maintaining your system. Regularly updating software ensures that you have the latest bug fixes, performance enhancements, and security patches. Most package managers offer a simple way to

update all installed software. For example, with APT on Debian-based systems, you can run:

bash
Copy

```bash
sudo apt update
```

10. `sudo apt upgrade`
11.

The `apt update` command refreshes the list of available packages, and `apt upgrade` upgrades all of the installed packages that have newer versions available. It's generally a good practice to run these commands regularly to keep your system secure and running efficiently.
Similarly, with YUM on Red Hat-based systems, you can run:

bash
Copy

```bash
sudo yum update
```

12.

If you prefer, you can update individual packages by specifying the package name:

bash
Copy

```bash
sudo apt install --only-upgrade <package-name>
```

13.

14. **Removing Software** is just as important as installing it. Over time, you may find that some software is no longer necessary. Removing unused or unnecessary software helps keep your system clean and frees up disk space. To remove a package using APT, you can run:

bash
Copy

```
sudo apt remove <package-name>
```

15.

This will remove the specified package, but leave behind any configuration files. If you want to remove the package along with its configuration files, use:
bash
Copy

```
sudo apt purge <package-name>
```

16.

Similarly, with YUM on Red Hat-based systems, you can remove a package with:
bash
Copy

```
sudo yum remove <package-name>
```

17.

18. **Cleaning Up After Software Removal** is important to ensure that your system doesn't accumulate unnecessary files over time. After removing a package, you might have residual configuration files or unused dependencies lingering on your system. Most package managers have commands to clean up these leftovers. With APT, you can use:
bash
Copy

```
sudo apt autoremove
```

19. ```sudo apt clean```

20.

The `autoremove` command removes packages that were automatically installed as dependencies but are no longer needed. The `clean` command clears out the local cache of downloaded packages, freeing up space.

Similarly, with YUM, you can use:

bash
Copy

```
sudo yum autoremove
```

21.

22. **Compiling Software from Source** is sometimes necessary when software isn't available via a package manager, or you need a custom build with specific features. Compiling from source involves downloading the source code, configuring it, compiling it, and installing it manually. While this process can be more complex, it offers flexibility and control over the software installation.

Here's a basic overview of the steps involved in compiling software from source:

- o   Download the source code, often in `.tar.gz` or `.tar.bz2` format.

- o   Extract the source code:
     bash
     Copy

     ```
     tar -xvf software.tar.gz
     ```

- o

- o   Navigate into the extracted directory:
     bash
     Copy

     ```
     cd software
     ```

- o

- o   Run the `configure` script, which checks your system for required libraries and dependencies:
     bash
     Copy

```
./configure
```

- o

- o Compile the software:
  ```bash
  ```
  `Copy`

  ```
  make
  ```

- o

- o Install the software:
  ```bash
  ```
  `Copy`

  ```
  sudo make install
  ```

- o

23. After installation, you can usually run the software directly from the terminal. However, keep in mind that when you install software from source, you must manually handle updates and dependencies.

24. **Managing Repositories** is an important part of managing software on Unix systems. Repositories are collections of software packages that are stored and made available by the software maintainers. By default, your package manager is configured to access a set of repositories, but you can add, remove, or change these repositories if you want to use different or custom sources for your software.

For example, on a Debian-based system, you can manage repositories by editing the `/etc/apt/sources.list` file, which contains a list of the repositories your system uses. You can add third-party repositories or mirror sites if you need specific versions of software not found in the default repositories.

On Red Hat-based systems, repository configuration files are stored in `/etc/yum.repos.d/`. You can add custom repository files here to use alternative sources for your software.

25. **Third-Party Package Managers** are also available for specific programming languages and environments. For instance, if you're a developer working with Python, you'll likely use **pip** (Python's package manager) to install Python libraries. Similarly, if you're working with Node.js, you'll use **npm** (Node Package Manager) to install JavaScript packages.

To install a Python package with `pip`, you'd run:

bash
Copy

```bash
pip install <package-name>
```

26.

For Node.js, to install a JavaScript package globally, use:

bash
Copy

```bash
npm install -g <package-name>
```

27.

These package managers work similarly to system package managers but are tailored for the specific language or environment.

28. **Security and Updates**: One of the most important aspects of software management is ensuring that your system is always up to date, especially when it comes to **security patches**. Many security vulnerabilities are discovered regularly in software, and updating packages is the most effective way to protect your system. Some package managers allow you to check for security-specific updates, and many modern systems will alert you to available updates. To ensure your system is always secure, enable automatic updates (where possible) and run regular update commands.

29. **Managing Software Versions** is an important aspect of software maintenance. If you need to install a specific version of a package, package managers often allow you to specify the version you want. For example, in APT, you can install a specific version of a package with:

bash
Copy

```bash
sudo apt install <package-name>=<version-number>
```

If you need to downgrade a package to a previous version, you can do so by specifying the version in the same manner.

31. **In conclusion**, managing software is a fundamental skill for every Unix user. Whether you're installing software with a package manager, compiling from source, or managing repositories, it's essential to keep your system's software up to date and properly configured. By using package managers like APT, YUM, or Pacman, you can streamline the process of maintaining your system's software, making it easier to install, update, and remove software as needed. Additionally, understanding the nuances of software management—such as managing repositories, compiling from source, and dealing with third-party package managers—will give you the flexibility to handle any situation. Keep your system's software fresh and secure, and you'll always be one step ahead!

Managing Software Dependencies is another critical aspect of Unix software management. Dependencies refer to the additional software libraries or packages required for a program to run. When you install a program, it often relies on other libraries or tools that must be installed beforehand. Package managers like APT and YUM usually handle dependencies automatically, but sometimes issues arise where dependencies are missing or incompatible.

To resolve these issues, package managers will often suggest solutions. For example, if you're installing a program with APT and missing dependencies, it will display messages prompting you to install them:

```bash
Copy
sudo apt install -f
```
This command attempts to fix any broken dependencies by automatically installing the required packages.

If you're working with software compiled from source, you might have to manually install the necessary libraries or tools. In such cases, it's important to keep track of your system's package dependencies to avoid conflicts and ensure everything is up to date.

Building a Local Package Repository is something you might need to do in an environment with limited or no internet access. This is especially relevant in enterprise settings or for isolated systems that don't have a direct connection to the internet. You can create a local repository that mirrors the software repositories for your distribution, making it easier to manage packages in offline environments.

Tools like **apt-mirror** (for APT-based systems) or **reposync** (for YUM-based systems) allow you to create your own repositories by downloading and syncing packages locally. Once the repository is created, you can configure your system to access this local repository, speeding up installation and updates without requiring an internet connection.

Software Snapshots and Rollbacks provide a way to undo changes when installing or updating software. Sometimes, after an update, a package may cause issues with your system, and you might need to revert to an older version. Many package managers provide a way to roll back updates or restore packages to previous versions.

For example, with **APT**, you can view available versions of a package using the following command:

```bash
apt list -a <package-name>
```

Then, to install a previous version, use:

```bash
sudo apt install <package-name>=<version-number>
```

Additionally, some Linux distributions use **system snapshots** (with tools like **timeshift** or **rsnapshot**) to take periodic backups of the system's state. These backups allow you to roll back your entire system to a previous configuration, effectively undoing any unwanted changes made by software updates or installations.

Automating Software Management with scripts is another powerful technique. For regular maintenance tasks, such as updating software, cleaning up unnecessary files, or checking for broken packages, you can write scripts to automate these tasks. Automation ensures that these tasks are performed consistently and on schedule, without the need for manual intervention.

For example, a simple script to update your system and remove unnecessary packages might look like this:

```bash
#!/bin/bash
sudo apt update
sudo apt upgrade -y
sudo apt autoremove -y
echo "System updated and cleaned."
```

You can then schedule this script to run regularly using **cron**, ensuring that your system stays up to date without you having to do anything manually.

Software Compatibility is something you'll need to consider when managing software on Unix. Sometimes, the latest version of a program might not be compatible with older versions of libraries or other software. This can happen when new software introduces features or changes that break compatibility with older versions.

To address compatibility issues, many package managers allow you to install specific versions of software or install both old and new versions alongside each other. Some distributions also provide **backports**, which are older versions of software that are updated and patched for use on newer systems, ensuring compatibility with the latest operating system versions.

Additionally, **containers** (like Docker) and **virtual machines** can be useful tools for running software in isolated environments where you can control dependencies and compatibility without affecting your main system.

Managing Software Licenses is another important aspect of software management, especially for organizations that use proprietary or commercial software. Many software packages are licensed under various licenses, and it's essential to track and manage these licenses to ensure compliance with legal requirements.

Some package managers, such as APT and YUM, allow you to view licensing information for installed software. Additionally, tools like **FOSSology** or **Black Duck** can help organizations track and manage open-source software licenses in their projects, ensuring compliance and avoiding potential legal pitfalls.

Software Security is an ongoing concern, and regular updates are essential for maintaining a secure system. Most package managers automatically download security updates, but in some cases, you might need to configure your system to ensure it receives security patches promptly. On Debian-based systems, you can enable **unattended-upgrades**, which automatically installs security updates:

bash
Copy
```bash
sudo apt install unattended-upgrades
```
Similarly, on Red Hat-based systems, you can configure **yum-cron** to automatically install security updates on a regular schedule.

Keeping your system secure means staying up to date with patches, regularly checking for vulnerabilities, and using security tools to scan for potential issues. Many security patches are released to address zero-day vulnerabilities or other critical issues, so ensuring timely updates is key to preventing attacks.

In conclusion, managing software on Unix systems is a dynamic and ongoing process. From installing and updating packages to managing dependencies and security, software management is a vital part of keeping your system running smoothly and securely. With tools like APT, YUM, Pacman, and others, you have the ability to easily manage your system's software, ensuring that you're always working with the latest and most secure versions. By automating updates, using version control, and staying on top of software security, you can maintain a reliable and efficient system that meets your needs. So, keep your system up to date, manage your software effectively, and ensure that your Unix system is always in optimal condition. Happy managing!

Chapter 18: System Monitoring: Keeping Your Eye on the Prize

1. As a Unix user or system administrator, **monitoring your system** is an essential skill. Just like a ship captain keeps an eye on the instruments to ensure the vessel is running smoothly, system monitoring allows you to track your Unix system's health and performance. Whether you're managing a personal machine, a server, or a large network, understanding how to monitor your system is key to maintaining its efficiency and security. In this chapter, we'll explore the tools and techniques you can use to keep a watchful eye on your system, ensuring that everything is running smoothly and that potential issues are caught before they become problems.

2. **Why monitor your system?** The answer is simple: to ensure optimal performance, avoid downtime, and address issues before they affect users or services. Monitoring helps you track resources like CPU, memory, disk usage, network traffic, and running processes, allowing you to identify bottlenecks, security risks, or hardware failures. Regular system monitoring can help you maintain system stability, avoid outages, and keep your Unix system in peak condition. Let's explore some of the key monitoring tools available on Unix systems.

3. **Top** is one of the most commonly used command-line tools for monitoring system performance. It provides a real-time, interactive view of the processes running on your system, showing resource usage for CPU, memory, and disk. To launch `top`, simply type:

bash
Copy

```
top
```

4.

The `top` command shows a constantly updating list of running processes, along with statistics on CPU and memory usage. You can sort the output by different criteria, such as CPU usage or memory usage, by pressing the corresponding key (e.g., P for CPU and M for memory).

5. A more modern and feature-rich alternative to `top` is **htop**. `htop` offers a more user-friendly, colorful, and interactive interface that displays system information in real-time. It's a more intuitive tool, allowing you to navigate through processes, view system stats, and even kill processes directly from the interface. To install `htop`, run:

bash
Copy

```
sudo apt install htop
```

6.

Once installed, simply type `htop` to start monitoring your system. The interface includes visual indicators for CPU, memory, and swap usage, and you can sort processes by various metrics.

7. **Free** is another simple but useful command for checking memory usage. It displays the total amount of RAM, used RAM, free RAM, and swap space. To check your system's memory usage, run:

bash
Copy

```
free -h
```

8.

The `-h` flag ensures that the output is in a human-readable format, showing sizes in MB or GB. This is an easy way to see if your system is running low on memory or if it's using too much swap space, which can be a sign of performance issues.

9. **Iostat** is an excellent tool for monitoring **disk usage and performance**. It provides information about CPU utilization and disk input/output operations. This tool is especially useful if you're trying to troubleshoot disk performance issues. To run `iostat`, use:

bash
Copy

```
iostat
```

10.

This will display statistics on CPU usage and I/O operations. You can also specify the interval at which the statistics are displayed. For example, to display statistics every 5 seconds, run:

bash
Copy

```
iostat 5
```

11.

12. **Vmstat** (Virtual Memory Statistics) provides a detailed view of your system's memory, processes, and system performance. Unlike `top` or `htop`, which focus on real-time process monitoring, `vmstat` focuses more on system-wide metrics like memory usage, paging, and disk I/O. To run `vmstat`, type:
bash
Copy

```
vmstat 1
```

13.

This will provide updates every second. It's particularly useful for diagnosing memory issues, such as excessive swapping or paging.

14. **Netstat** is a useful tool for monitoring **network connections**. It provides information about your system's network interfaces, routing tables, and active network connections. To check for open network ports and active connections, use:
bash
Copy

```
netstat -tuln
```

15.

The `-tuln` flags show TCP (`-t`) and UDP (`-u`) connections that are in a listening state (`-l`) without resolving hostnames (`-n`). You can also use `netstat` to view detailed routing information with:
bash
Copy

```
netstat -r
```

16.

17. **Nmap** is another great tool for network monitoring, especially if you want to scan your network or check for open ports on remote systems. You can use `nmap` to scan local or remote networks to find active devices, open ports, and potential vulnerabilities. To scan your local network for open ports, run:

bash
Copy

```
nmap -sP 192.168.1.0/24
```

18.

This command performs a ping scan of the `192.168.1.0/24` subnet, listing all live hosts. `Nmap` also allows for more advanced scanning options, including service version detection and OS fingerprinting.

19. **Sar (System Activity Reporter)** is a comprehensive tool for collecting and displaying performance metrics over time. Unlike the real-time nature of tools like `top` or `htop`, `sar` collects data in the background, allowing you to review past performance over a period of time. To view CPU activity from the last 24 hours, you can run:

bash
Copy

```
sar -u 1 10
```

20.

This will show CPU usage statistics every second for the last 10 intervals. Sar can be used to track long-term performance trends and identify problems that may have developed over time.

21. **System Logs** are invaluable when troubleshooting system performance and diagnosing issues. Unix systems log a wide variety of information, from system events and security alerts to hardware failures and software errors. The primary log files are stored in the `/var/log/` directory. Some important log files to keep an eye on include:

   ○ `/var/log/syslog` – General system log

   ○ `/var/log/auth.log` – Authentication log (user logins, sudo usage)

   ○ `/var/log/kern.log` – Kernel log (hardware issues, system errors)

- ○ `/var/log/dmesg` – Boot messages and kernel diagnostics

22. You can use `tail` to view the most recent entries in these logs. For example:
bash
Copy


```
tail -f /var/log/syslog
```

23.

This command continuously updates the log output in real-time, allowing you to monitor system events as they happen.

24. **Monitoring System Resources Remotely** is a critical aspect of managing servers or other remote systems. Tools like **SSH**, combined with system monitoring tools, allow you to keep an eye on your server's health without being physically present. You can run commands like `top`, `htop`, and `free` over SSH to check the system's resource usage. For more advanced remote monitoring, you can use tools like **Nagios** or **Zabbix**, which provide centralized monitoring of multiple systems, sending alerts if something goes wrong. These tools are particularly useful for large-scale networked systems and provide automated notification systems.

25. **Disk Usage Monitoring** is essential for ensuring that your system doesn't run out of space, which could cause application crashes or performance degradation. The **df** command shows the available space on your mounted file systems. For example, to check disk space usage, run:
bash
Copy


```
df -h
```

26.

The `-h` flag displays the output in a human-readable format (MB, GB, etc.). If you want to check the disk usage of individual directories or files, you can use the `du` (disk usage) command:
bash
Copy

27.
```
du -sh /path/to/directory
```

This will show the total disk usage of the specified directory.

28. Alerting and Notification is an essential part of proactive system monitoring. Setting up alerts allows you to receive notifications when certain thresholds are reached, such as CPU usage going over 90%, or disk space running low. Tools like **Nagios**, **Zabbix**, or **Prometheus** can be configured to send emails or messages through Slack or other channels when specific conditions are met.

29. In conclusion, system monitoring is not just about keeping an eye on your system—it's about understanding your system's health and performance, diagnosing issues, and ensuring that everything runs smoothly. With the right tools in place, you can monitor resource usage, identify bottlenecks, and troubleshoot problems before they affect your users. By regularly checking logs, using commands like `top`, `htop`, and `netstat`, and configuring automated alerts, you'll be able to manage your system with confidence. System monitoring is an ongoing task that pays dividends in system stability, performance, and security. Keep your eye on the prize, and your system will reward you with uptime, speed, and reliability!

Automation in System Monitoring can greatly reduce the need for manual checks, making it easier to maintain consistent oversight of your system's health. By scripting common monitoring tasks, you can automate things like checking disk usage, CPU load, and memory usage, and even set up scheduled reports that summarize system performance over time. For example, you could create a simple script to check for disk space usage every day and email you if it's over a certain threshold. A basic script could look like this:

```bash
Copy
#!/bin/bash
# Check disk usage and send email if usage is over 90%
THRESHOLD=90
EMAIL="youremail@example.com"

usage=$(df / | grep / | awk '{ print $5 }' | sed 's/%//g')

if [ $usage -gt $THRESHOLD ]; then
    echo "Disk space usage is over $THRESHOLD%. Current
usage: $usage%" | mail -s "Disk space warning" $EMAIL
fi
```

This script uses `df` to check disk usage on the root directory, compares it with a defined threshold, and sends an email alert if the threshold is exceeded. Automating such tasks ensures that you're promptly informed of any issues without needing to constantly monitor your system manually.

Cloud-based Monitoring is becoming increasingly popular as more organizations move to the cloud. Tools like **CloudWatch** (for AWS), **Azure Monitor**, and **Google Cloud Operations** provide cloud-native monitoring solutions that allow you to manage both cloud-based and on-premises systems in one place. These tools typically offer robust dashboards, real-time metrics, and alerting capabilities that can be customized for your environment. For example, CloudWatch lets you monitor EC2 instances, RDS databases, and Lambda functions, giving you insight into your cloud-based infrastructure. Integrating your Unix monitoring tools with cloud platforms can provide comprehensive visibility into your entire infrastructure.

Performance Tuning is a vital part of system monitoring. Identifying performance bottlenecks is key to improving the efficiency and responsiveness of your Unix system. If you notice that processes are using excessive CPU or memory, it might be time to look into performance tuning. One important tool for performance tuning is `sysctl`, which allows you to modify kernel parameters at runtime. For example, you can check your system's current kernel parameters with:

bash
Copy
```
sysctl -a
```
And change specific parameters, like the maximum number of open files allowed, with:

bash
Copy
```
sudo sysctl -w fs.file-max=100000
```
Performance tuning can help prevent problems before they occur and ensure that your system operates at peak efficiency.

Understanding Logs and Their Role in Monitoring is crucial for diagnosing problems and understanding the overall health of your system. System logs contain a wealth of information, ranging from system startup messages to kernel errors and application-specific logs. Learning how to parse and analyze these logs will make you much more effective at system monitoring. Tools like `journalctl` (for systems using `systemd`) allow you to query logs from various services in real-time, providing insight into what's happening on your system. For example:

bash
Copy
```
journalctl -u nginx.service
```
This command will show the logs for the `nginx` web server service, allowing you to quickly diagnose issues specific to that service. You can also use `grep` in conjunction with log files to find specific patterns, such as error messages or warnings:

bash
Copy

```
grep "error" /var/log/syslog
```
Real-time Monitoring Tools like **Grafana**, **Prometheus**, and **Netdata** can give you powerful, visual representations of your system's performance metrics. These tools collect data from your system and display it on interactive dashboards, allowing you to easily track metrics over time. For example, Prometheus can be set up to gather metrics from your system and various services, and then Grafana can be used to visualize this data, offering you real-time performance insights. These tools are especially useful for managing larger systems, where manually checking system stats with commands like `top` and `netstat` is not practical.

Custom Alerts and Thresholds are essential for proactive system monitoring. Many monitoring tools allow you to define custom thresholds that trigger alerts when a specific condition is met. For instance, you could set up an alert to notify you when CPU usage exceeds 85%, or when disk usage is over 90%. Setting these thresholds ensures that you are immediately informed of potential issues and can take action before they escalate. Monitoring tools such as **Nagios**, **Zabbix**, and **Prometheus** offer this capability, and you can customize the thresholds based on the particular needs of your environment.

Automated Recovery should also be part of your monitoring strategy. While it's great to be alerted to problems, it's even better to have systems in place that can recover from common issues automatically. For example, if a critical service like a web server goes down, you could configure a script to restart the service automatically. Many modern monitoring tools, like **Monit** or **systemd's service monitoring** capabilities, can help automate service recovery. With systemd, you can set it to automatically restart a service if it fails:

```bash
Copy
[Service]
Restart=always
```
This configuration ensures that the service will be restarted automatically if it crashes, reducing downtime and the need for manual intervention.

System Monitoring and Security are tightly linked. By monitoring your system, you not only keep an eye on performance but also safeguard your system against potential security breaches. Monitoring system logs, network traffic, and user activity can help you detect signs of unauthorized access or malicious activity. Tools like **Fail2ban** can help monitor login attempts and automatically block IP addresses that are making too many failed attempts. Additionally, tools like **auditd** (the audit daemon) can track system calls and events to help identify suspicious behavior on the system.

In conclusion, system monitoring is a critical aspect of maintaining any Unix-based system, whether it's a personal machine, a server, or a large-scale network. With the right tools and practices in place, you can ensure your system runs efficiently, stays secure, and performs optimally. From tools like `top` and `htop` for real-time performance tracking, to advanced solutions like Prometheus and Grafana for visualizing system data, the options available to you are vast. By setting up regular monitoring routines, automating alerts and recovery, and using logging and threshold tools, you'll be able to keep your system in top shape. So, keep your eye on the prize—your system's health—and use the power of Unix to ensure everything stays running smoothly. Happy monitoring!

Chapter 19: Security 101: Locking Down Your Unix Fortress

1. In today's digital world, **security** is not just a consideration—it's a necessity. Just as you wouldn't leave your house unlocked or your valuables unguarded, you shouldn't leave your Unix system unprotected. Whether you're running a personal laptop, managing a server, or overseeing a network of machines, securing your system is paramount to preventing unauthorized access, data loss, and attacks. In this chapter, we'll explore the fundamentals of Unix security, covering everything from user management to firewall configuration and network protection. With the right tools and practices, you can lock down your Unix system like a fortress.

2. **User and Permission Management** is the foundation of Unix security. Unix systems have a robust user management system, where each user is assigned unique permissions that define what they can and cannot do. By managing users and permissions carefully, you can restrict access to sensitive files and ensure that only authorized users can perform certain actions.
   To view the current users on the system, you can use:

   bash
   Copy

   ```
   cat /etc/passwd
   ```

3.

   This file contains a list of all users, along with their default shell, home directory, and other information. When creating new users, it's essential to assign them only the permissions they need to perform their tasks. Avoid using the root user for daily activities, and instead, create specific users with limited privileges.

4. **User Groups** allow you to manage permissions more efficiently. Instead of assigning permissions to individual users, you can group users together and assign permissions to the entire group. For example, if you have several users who need access to the same directory, you can create a group and grant the group access. To create a new group, use the `groupadd` command:

   bash
   Copy

   ```
   sudo groupadd developers
   ```

5.

You can then add users to this group with the `usermod` command:
bash
Copy

```
sudo usermod -aG developers user1
```
6.

This command adds `user1` to the `developers` group, allowing them to access resources that are accessible to the group. Always be mindful of group membership, as it determines who has access to shared resources.

7. **File Permissions** in Unix are essential for controlling who can read, write, and execute files. Each file has three types of permissions: **read (r)**, **write (w)**, and **execute (x)**. These permissions are assigned to the **owner**, **group**, and **others**. You can view the permissions of a file with the `ls -l` command:
bash
Copy

```
ls -l filename
```

8.

The output will show something like:
diff
Copy

```
-rwxr-xr--
```
9.

This means that the owner can read, write, and execute the file, the group can read and execute, and others can only read the file. You can modify file permissions using the `chmod` command. For example, to give the group write permission, use:
bash

```
chmod g+w filename
```

10.

Similarly, you can change the ownership of a file using the `chown` command:
bash

```
sudo chown user1:developers filename
```

11.

This ensures that the file is owned by `user1` and belongs to the `developers` group.

12. **Sudo and Root Access** are two of the most powerful tools in Unix, but they should be used with caution. The `sudo` command allows a user to execute commands with elevated privileges, while the root user has complete control over the system. It's essential to limit the use of `sudo` to only trusted users, as this grants them administrative privileges. When configuring `sudo` access, always follow the principle of **least privilege**, only granting users the minimal permissions required for their tasks.
The `sudoers` file determines who can use `sudo`. To edit this file, use the `visudo` command:
bash

```
sudo visudo
```

13.

Here, you can add users and specify which commands they are allowed to run with `sudo`.

14. **Password Management** is one of the most critical aspects of Unix security. Weak or easily guessable passwords are a significant vulnerability. To create strong passwords, ensure they contain a mix of uppercase and lowercase letters, numbers, and special characters, and are at least 12 characters long. You can enforce password strength policies using the `/etc/login.defs` file or by using the `pam_pwquality` module in PAM (Pluggable Authentication Modules).

To force password expiration and regular updates, you can use the `chage` command:

bash

Copy

```
sudo chage -M 30 username
```

15.

This command forces the user to change their password every 30 days. Additionally, consider setting up **two-factor authentication** (2FA) to add an extra layer of security to user accounts.

16. **SSH Security** is another critical area. SSH is widely used for remote logins, and while it's secure by default, you can make it even more secure by configuring certain settings. One of the first steps is to disable **root login** via SSH. To do this, edit the `/etc/ssh/sshd_config` file:

bash

Copy

```
sudo nano /etc/ssh/sshd_config
```

17.

Set the following line to `no`:

bash

Copy

```
PermitRootLogin no
```

18.

This ensures that the root account cannot be accessed remotely, forcing users to log in with individual user accounts. You should also consider using **SSH key-based authentication** instead of password-based authentication for enhanced security. This can be done by generating an SSH key pair using:

bash

Copy

19.

```
ssh-keygen -t rsa
```

Then, copy the public key to the remote server:
bash
Copy

20.

```
ssh-copy-id user@remote-server
```

21. Firewalls are essential for protecting your Unix system from unwanted network traffic. A firewall can help block unauthorized access and filter traffic based on IP addresses, ports, and protocols. One of the most commonly used tools for configuring a firewall in Unix is **iptables** (or **ufw** for Ubuntu). To view the current firewall rules, run:
bash
Copy

22.

```
sudo iptables -L
```

To add a rule that blocks all incoming traffic except for SSH (port 22), use:
bash
Copy

23.
24.

```
sudo iptables -A INPUT -p tcp --dport 22 -j ACCEPT
sudo iptables -A INPUT -j DROP
```

This will allow SSH connections while blocking all other incoming traffic. If you're using **ufw**, the command would look like:
bash
Copy

```
   sudo ufw allow ssh
```

25. `sudo ufw enable`
26.

27. **Audit Logging** is an essential tool for monitoring and securing your system. Unix systems generate logs for various activities, including login attempts, system events, and file access. Configuring and reviewing audit logs allows you to detect unauthorized access or suspicious behavior. The **auditd** service (Audit Daemon) provides detailed logs of system activity, including user commands and system calls.
To install and enable auditd on Ubuntu, run:
bash
Copy

```
   sudo apt install auditd
```

28. `sudo systemctl start auditd`
29. `sudo systemctl enable auditd`
30.

You can configure rules to track specific files, directories, or commands by editing `/etc/audit/audit.rules`.

31. **Software Updates and Security Patches** are essential to keeping your system secure. Vulnerabilities in software can be exploited by attackers, so keeping everything up to date is crucial. Most Unix-based systems have package managers that make it easy to apply security patches. For example, on Debian-based systems, use:
bash
Copy

```
   sudo apt update
```

32. `sudo apt upgrade`
33.

On Red Hat-based systems, use:
bash

```
sudo yum update
```

34.

Regularly updating your system ensures that security patches and bug fixes are applied, protecting your system from new threats.

35. **In conclusion**, securing a Unix system requires a multi-layered approach that includes user management, file permissions, password policies, SSH security, firewalls, and software updates. By taking the time to configure and monitor these security features, you can significantly reduce the risk of unauthorized access and maintain a secure environment. Implementing best practices like limiting root access, using SSH key-based authentication, and keeping your system updated will help you lock down your Unix fortress. Security is an ongoing process—so continue learning, stay vigilant, and keep your Unix system safe from threats.

Security Auditing is an essential practice in maintaining a secure Unix system. Regular audits allow you to proactively check for vulnerabilities, ensure that best security practices are followed, and verify that your system's configuration is in line with your security policies. Tools like **Lynis** can help perform a security audit on your system, checking for vulnerabilities and offering suggestions for improvements. To install and run Lynis, use:

bash
```
sudo apt install lynis
sudo lynis audit system
```
Lynis will run a comprehensive security scan of your system, highlighting potential issues and areas for improvement. It's an invaluable tool for ensuring your Unix system is secure and compliant with industry standards.

Intrusion Detection Systems (IDS) are a critical component in advanced Unix security setups. An IDS monitors your system for suspicious activity or potential attacks, and can alert you when something abnormal happens, such as a brute-force login attempt or unauthorized file access. **Fail2ban** is one such tool that works well with SSH and other services to protect against brute-force attacks by blocking IP addresses after a certain number of failed login attempts. To install Fail2ban on Ubuntu:

bash
```
sudo apt install fail2ban
```
Fail2ban automatically updates firewall rules to block attackers and helps protect against common network intrusion techniques.

Disabling Unused Services is another crucial step in securing your system. Many Unix systems run several services by default, some of which may not be necessary for your needs. Every additional service is another potential vector for an attack, so disabling unnecessary services reduces your system's exposure. To list all running services, you can use:

bash
Copy

```
sudo systemctl list-units --type=service
```

To disable a service that isn't required, such as the **telnet** service (which is insecure), use:

bash
Copy

```
sudo systemctl stop telnet
sudo systemctl disable telnet
```

Always review the services running on your system and disable any that are unnecessary or insecure.

Securing the Boot Process is another important aspect of Unix security. If an attacker has physical access to your machine, they could attempt to manipulate your system before it even boots. You can secure your boot process by setting a password for the GRUB bootloader to prevent unauthorized users from modifying boot options. To set a password for GRUB on Ubuntu, follow these steps:

1. First, create a password hash:
   bash
   Copy

   ```
   grub-mkpasswd-pbkdf2
   ```

2.

3. Then, add the hash to the GRUB configuration file:
   bash
   Copy

   ```
   sudo nano /etc/grub.d/40_custom
   ```

4.

Add the following lines to the file:

```bash
```
Copy
```
set superusers="root"
password_pbkdf2 root <password-hash>
```
   3. Update GRUB to apply the changes:
```bash
```
Copy

```
sudo update-grub
```

   4.

This ensures that only authorized users can make changes to the boot process, securing your system against tampering at startup.

Encryption is a powerful tool for protecting data on your Unix system. Whether you're dealing with sensitive personal information or corporate data, encryption ensures that your files remain private, even if your system is compromised. There are two primary types of encryption you should consider:

- **Full Disk Encryption (FDE)**: Encrypts the entire disk, protecting all files on the system. This is particularly useful for laptops and mobile devices that may be lost or stolen. Tools like **LUKS (Linux Unified Key Setup)** can be used to encrypt your entire hard drive during installation or after the fact.

- **File Encryption**: For sensitive files, you can use tools like **GPG (GNU Privacy Guard)** to encrypt files individually. To encrypt a file with GPG, use:
```bash
```
Copy

```
gpg -c sensitivefile.txt
```

-

   This will create an encrypted version of the file, which can only be decrypted using a password.

Network Security is a top priority for Unix system administrators, especially if your system is connected to the internet. Setting up and configuring firewalls is one of the first steps in securing your network. **iptables** or **firewalld** (on systems using `systemd`) are commonly used to define rules that control the flow of traffic into and out of your system. A basic iptables rule to block all incoming connections except for SSH looks like this:

```bash
Copy
sudo iptables -A INPUT -p tcp --dport 22 -j ACCEPT
sudo iptables -A INPUT -j DROP
```
Always configure your firewall to allow only necessary traffic and regularly check which ports are open on your system to prevent unauthorized access.

Backup Strategies are crucial to ensuring the security of your data. In case of a system breach, data loss, or hardware failure, having secure backups allows you to restore your system to its previous state. You should use **encrypted backups** and store them in a **remote location** (such as a cloud service or a remote server) to ensure they are protected against physical theft and cyberattacks.

Tools like **rsync** and **tar** can help you create regular, automated backups. Here's a simple command to back up your home directory to a remote server:

```bash
Copy
rsync -avz /home/user user@remote-server:/backup/
```
Make sure your backup process includes regular testing to verify that your backup files are restorable.

Security Best Practices should always be followed to maintain a robust defense against potential threats. These include:

- **Using SSH keys instead of passwords** for remote access.

- **Regularly reviewing logs** for unusual activity, particularly authentication logs.

- **Regularly updating your system** and installed software to patch security vulnerabilities.

- **Disabling unused ports** and services.

- **Setting up security alerts** for unusual events or failures.

- **Educating users** on safe practices, such as recognizing phishing attempts or not reusing passwords.

In conclusion, securing a Unix system is an ongoing process that requires vigilance, careful configuration, and proactive measures. From controlling user access and managing file permissions to implementing encryption and firewall rules, there are many layers of security you can apply to your system. Regularly updating your system, monitoring logs, and conducting security audits will help keep potential threats at bay. By following these security best practices, you can create a solid defense against attacks and ensure the safety of your data and systems.

Treat your Unix machine like a fortress—harden it, protect it, and make sure it's always on guard. Happy securing!

Chapter 20: Advanced Scripting: A Masterpiece in the Making

1. As you've learned in previous chapters, Unix scripting is one of the most powerful ways to automate tasks and interact with your system. But just as an artist refines their craft to create masterpieces, you too can elevate your scripting skills to a level where your scripts are not only functional but also elegant, efficient, and powerful. In this chapter, we'll dive into **advanced scripting techniques**, covering everything from using functions and loops to handling complex data structures and incorporating error handling. By the end of this chapter, you'll have the tools and knowledge to write scripts that can solve complex problems and run reliably in any environment.

2. **Functions** are the building blocks of advanced scripts. A function is simply a block of reusable code that performs a specific task. Functions allow you to organize your scripts into logical sections, making them easier to read, maintain, and reuse. For example, consider the following simple function that greets the user:

   bash
   Copy

   ```
   greet_user() {
   ```

3. ```
           echo "Hello, $1!"
   ```
4. ```
   }
   ```
5.

   Here, `greet_user` is a function that takes one argument (`$1`), which is the user's name, and prints a greeting. You can call this function by simply passing the user's name as an argument:

   bash
   Copy

   ```
   greet_user John
   ```
6.

   Functions make your scripts modular and allow you to avoid repeating the same code in different places. They're an essential tool for creating more complex and structured scripts.

7. **Return Values** are a key aspect of functions. In addition to performing a task, functions can also return values that can be used by other parts of your script. In Unix scripting, functions don't technically return values like in some other programming languages (such as Python or JavaScript). Instead, they typically return an **exit status** (0 for success, 1 for failure) or output through `echo`. For example:

bash
Copy

```
sum_numbers() {
```

8.   `echo $(($1 + $2))`
9. `}`
10.
11. `result=$(sum_numbers 5 7)`
12. `echo "The sum is: $result"`
13.

Here, the `sum_numbers` function takes two arguments, adds them together, and prints the result. The script then captures the output and stores it in the `result` variable for later use. Using `echo` in your functions allows you to easily return values.

14. **Loops** are another essential tool for handling repetitive tasks in your scripts. While simple loops like `for` and `while` might seem basic, they become incredibly powerful when combined with conditionals and functions. For example, let's say you want to loop through a list of files and check if they exist:

bash
Copy

```
files=("file1.txt" "file2.txt" "file3.txt")
```

15.
16. `for file in "${files[@]}"; do`
17.   `if [[ -e $file ]]; then`
18.   `echo "$file exists."`
19.   `else`
20.   `echo "$file does not exist."`
21.   `fi`
22. `done`

23.

In this script, the `for` loop iterates over an array of filenames and checks whether each file exists using an `if` statement. Loops allow you to automate tasks that would otherwise require manual effort, and combining them with conditionals lets you handle complex logic within your scripts.

24. **Arrays** are another powerful feature of Unix scripts that allow you to store multiple values in a single variable. Arrays are useful when you need to work with collections of data. For example, let's say you want to create an array of directory names and then loop through each one to check if it exists:

bash
Copy

```
directories=("dir1" "dir2" "dir3")
```

25.
26. `for dir in "${directories[@]}"; do`
27. `    if [[ -d $dir ]]; then`
28. `        echo "$dir is a valid directory."`
29. `    else`
30. `        echo "$dir is not a valid directory."`
31. `    fi`
32. `done`
33.

Here, we've used an array to store a list of directories and looped through them to check whether each directory exists. Arrays in Unix scripting are indexed, meaning you can easily access or modify the elements by referencing their index (e.g., `${directories[0]}`).

34. **Associative Arrays** are another advanced feature that allows you to store key-value pairs in an array. Unlike regular arrays, which use numerical indices, associative arrays let you define your own keys, making them ideal for situations where you need to associate data with specific labels. Here's an example:

bash
Copy

```
declare -A user_info
```

```bash
35. user_info["name"]="Alice"
36. user_info["age"]="30"
37. user_info["location"]="Wonderland"
38.
39. echo "Name: ${user_info["name"]}"
40. echo "Age: ${user_info["age"]}"
41. echo "Location: ${user_info["location"]}"
42.
```

In this script, we use an associative array to store the user's name, age, and location, and then access the data using the keys ("name", "age", "location"). Associative arrays make your scripts more flexible and allow you to work with more complex data structures.

43. **Error Handling** is a critical part of any advanced script. Without error handling, your scripts can break or behave unexpectedly when something goes wrong. Unix provides several ways to handle errors. For example, you can check the exit status of a command using $?, which returns the exit code of the last executed command. A non-zero exit code indicates an error. Let's take a look at a simple script that checks if a file exists:

bash
Copy

```bash
check_file() {

44.     if [[ ! -f $1 ]]; then
45.         echo "Error: $1 does not exist."
46.         exit 1
47.     fi
48. }
49.
50. check_file "important_file.txt"
51.
```

In this script, the **check_file** function checks if the specified file exists. If it doesn't, the script prints an error message and exits with a non-zero exit code. Using exit 1 helps indicate that something went wrong, and this can be useful for troubleshooting and preventing further execution of the script.

52. **Trap** is a powerful command that allows you to handle signals and cleanup tasks in your scripts. For example, if a user presses Ctrl+C to interrupt the script, the script may not properly clean up temporary files or processes. By using trap, you can handle this

interruption and ensure that cleanup happens. Here's an example:
bash
Copy

```
cleanup() {
```

53.   echo "Cleaning up before exit..."
54.   rm -f /tmp/tempfile
55. }
56.
57. trap cleanup EXIT
58.
59. # Simulate a process
60. echo "Starting process..."
61. sleep 5
62.

In this script, the `cleanup` function is set to run when the script exits (due to either a successful completion or an interruption). This ensures that any temporary files are removed, preventing clutter and leaving your system clean.

63. **Debugging** is a crucial part of developing advanced scripts. While it can be frustrating, debugging allows you to identify and fix issues, ensuring your scripts run smoothly. One useful tool for debugging is `set -x`, which enables a trace of each command executed in the script. For example:
bash
Copy

```
#!/bin/bash
```

64. set -x
65.
66. echo "This is a debugged script"
67.

This will print each command to the terminal before executing it, helping you trace where things go wrong. You can also use `set -e` to make your script exit immediately if any command fails, making debugging easier.

68. **Regular Expressions (Regex)** are essential when you need to work with patterns in strings, such as finding specific words or validating input. Unix provides several tools that support regular expressions, such as `grep`, `sed`, and `awk`. For example, to search for lines containing "error" in a log file, you can use `grep` with a regular expression:

`bash`
Copy

```
grep -E "error|fail" logfile.txt
```

69.

The `-E` flag enables extended regular expressions, allowing you to search for multiple patterns (in this case, "error" or "fail"). Mastering regex is a valuable skill when working with text data in Unix scripts.

70. **In conclusion**, advanced scripting in Unix is about mastering the tools at your disposal and using them to create powerful, flexible, and efficient scripts. By understanding functions, loops, arrays, error handling, debugging, and regular expressions, you can write scripts that are not only functional but also well-structured and scalable. Whether you're automating tasks, processing data, or managing system configurations, advanced scripting allows you to do more with less effort. As you continue to practice and refine your skills, you'll find that scripting in Unix becomes not just a necessity but a masterpiece of your own making. Happy scripting!

Advanced Input and Output Handling is another important aspect of sophisticated Unix scripting. The ability to manipulate input and output efficiently can make your scripts more powerful. A key concept in Unix is the **pipeline**, which allows you to chain multiple commands together, sending the output of one command directly to the input of another. This enables complex tasks to be performed in a single line.

For example, you can combine `grep` with `awk` to search for a specific pattern and then process the results:

`bash`
Copy
```
cat file.txt | grep "pattern" | awk '{print $2, $3}'
```
This command first filters lines containing "pattern" and then extracts and prints the second and third columns of those lines. Pipelines are incredibly useful for processing large volumes of data and performing multiple operations in sequence.

File Descriptors are a concept that many advanced scripters use to handle input and output in more flexible ways. Unix provides three standard file descriptors: `stdin` (standard input), stdout (standard output), and stderr (standard error). By redirecting these file descriptors, you can control where input comes from and where output goes.

For example, you can redirect stdout to a file:

```bash
Copy
echo "Hello, World!" > output.txt
```

You can also redirect stderr to a file:

```bash
Copy
ls non_existent_directory 2> error_log.txt
```

You can combine both stdout and stderr:

```bash
Copy
command > output.txt 2>&1
```

This redirects both the standard output and the standard error to output.txt. Understanding file descriptors gives you more control over how your scripts interact with files and error handling.

Command Substitution allows you to use the output of one command as the input for another, which is an essential feature for advanced scripts. You can use command substitution in scripts to execute commands and capture their output. There are two syntaxes for command substitution:

- Backticks (old syntax):
  ```bash
  Copy
  
  result=`date`
  ```

-

- Dollar parentheses (modern syntax):
  ```bash
  Copy
  
  result=$(date)
  ```

The modern `$( )` syntax is preferred, as it's more readable and supports nested commands. For example, you can combine `date` with `echo` to print a message with the current date:

bash
Copy
```bash
echo "Today's date is: $(date)"
```
Command substitution makes it easy to include the results of system commands or calculations directly into your scripts.

Signal Handling is an advanced scripting feature that allows you to control how your script responds to signals. Signals are notifications sent to processes to inform them of events, such as an interruption (Ctrl+C) or a request to terminate. By using the `trap` command, you can specify how your script should handle certain signals.

For example, to handle the `SIGINT` signal (generated by pressing Ctrl+C) and perform cleanup before exiting, you can use:

bash
Copy
```bash
trap 'echo "Caught SIGINT, cleaning up..."; exit' SIGINT
```
This command ensures that when the script is interrupted, it will print a message and perform any necessary cleanup (such as removing temporary files) before exiting. Signals are critical for managing how your scripts behave in response to user actions or system events.

Parallel Processing in Unix allows you to run multiple processes simultaneously, making your scripts more efficient when dealing with tasks that can be performed in parallel. The `&` operator is used to run a command in the background:

bash
Copy
```bash
long_running_command &
```
To wait for all background jobs to finish, use the `wait` command:

bash
Copy
```bash
wait
```
For more advanced parallelism, you can use tools like **GNU Parallel**, which allows you to execute jobs in parallel and control the number of jobs run at once. For example:

bash
Copy
```bash
parallel echo ::: A B C D
```

This will run four instances of the `echo` command in parallel, printing A, B, C, and D simultaneously. Parallel processing is particularly useful when working with large datasets or when performing tasks that can be split into smaller parts.

Logging and Debugging are vital for any script that will be used in production or by others. By logging events, errors, and important information, you can track the behavior of your script and identify issues more easily. Using logging libraries or simply writing messages to a log file can make your script much more robust.

Here's an example of how you might implement logging in your script:

```bash
log_file="/var/log/myscript.log"

log_message() {
    echo "$(date) - $1" >> $log_file
}

log_message "Script started"
```

This function appends a log entry with the current date and time to the `myscript.log` file. Logging ensures that you can track your script's actions and helps with troubleshooting when something goes wrong.

Modular Scripts are a hallmark of high-quality Unix scripting. As your scripts grow in complexity, you'll want to divide them into smaller, more manageable pieces. Modular scripts make it easier to maintain, debug, and reuse parts of your script in different contexts.

For example, you could create a series of functions for different tasks, such as database backups, log file analysis, and sending email notifications. By grouping related functions into separate files and calling them from a central script, you can create reusable, maintainable code that is easier to update and test.

Here's an example of modularity in action:

```bash
# backup.sh
backup_data() {
    echo "Backing up data..."
}

# main.sh
source backup.sh
```

```
backup_data
```
In this example, the `main.sh` script imports the `backup.sh` script and calls the `backup_data` function. Modular scripts keep your code organized and reusable, allowing for better long-term maintenance.

Using External Libraries and Tools is another advanced scripting technique that allows you to leverage the power of existing Unix tools in your scripts. Many powerful utilities, like `awk`, `sed`, `grep`, `curl`, and `jq`, can be incorporated into your scripts to process data, perform transformations, or interact with external APIs.

For example, if you need to parse JSON data in your script, you can use `jq`:

bash
Copy
```bash
curl -s https://api.example.com/data | jq '.results[] | .name'
```
By using these tools, you can extend the functionality of your scripts without reinventing the wheel, making your code more efficient and powerful.

In conclusion, advanced scripting in Unix is about taking the foundational knowledge you've learned and refining it to create efficient, modular, and powerful scripts. By mastering functions, loops, error handling, file descriptors, and more, you can create scripts that automate complex tasks, perform data processing, and manage system resources. The skills and techniques covered in this chapter allow you to move from writing simple one-off scripts to crafting full-fledged, production-grade automation solutions. Keep practicing, experimenting, and refining your scripts, and soon you'll be writing Unix scripts that are not only functional but works of art. Happy scripting!

Chapter 21: Mounting and Unmounting: What's on Your Drive?

1. In the world of Unix, **mounting** and **unmounting** drives is a critical skill that every user and system administrator must understand. Whether you're working with local hard drives, external storage devices, or networked file systems, the process of mounting and unmounting determines how your system interacts with storage. In this chapter, we'll explore the concepts of mounting and unmounting in depth, covering everything from mounting physical drives to working with network file systems. By the end of this chapter, you'll have a firm grasp on managing storage devices and ensuring that data is accessible or safely disconnected when needed.

2. **What does "mounting" mean?** In Unix, "mounting" is the process of making a storage device (like a hard drive, USB flash drive, or network share) accessible to the operating system. When a storage device is mounted, it is assigned to a directory in the filesystem hierarchy, known as a **mount point**. This allows you to access files and directories on that device just like you would with files on your main system drive. The opposite of

mounting is **unmounting**, which safely detaches the storage device from the filesystem, ensuring that data is not corrupted when the device is removed.

3. **Mounting Local Drives** is typically done automatically by your Unix system during boot. For example, the root filesystem (`/`) and other important directories are usually mounted at startup based on entries in the `/etc/fstab` file. However, you may also need to manually mount external drives, CD-ROMs, or network shares.

   To mount a local drive, you need to know the device name (e.g., `/dev/sda1` for a typical hard drive partition) and the directory where you want to mount it (the mount point). For instance, to mount a drive to `/mnt`, you would use:

   bash
   Copy

   ```
   sudo mount /dev/sda1 /mnt
   ```

4.

   This command mounts the partition `/dev/sda1` to the `/mnt` directory, making the files on that partition accessible at `/mnt`.

5. **Identifying Devices to Mount**: Before you can mount a drive, you need to know which devices are available on your system. The **lsblk** command is a great way to list all block devices (i.e., drives and partitions) on your system. For example:

   bash
   Copy

   ```
   lsblk
   ```

6.

   This will display a list of devices, including their mount points (if mounted), sizes, and types. The output might look something like:

   bash
   Copy

   ```
   NAME     MAJ:MIN  RM    SIZE RO TYPE MOUNTPOINT
   ```

7. `sda      8:0      0   1000G  0 disk`
8. `├─sda1   8:1      0    500G  0 part /mnt`

9. └─sda2   8:2   0   500G   0 part /data
10.

In this example, two partitions (`/dev/sda1` and `/dev/sda2`) are on the device `/dev/sda`. Each partition has its own mount point (`/mnt` and `/data`, respectively).

11. **File Systems** are an essential concept when working with mounting. Each storage device is formatted with a file system that determines how data is stored and accessed. Common file systems include **ext4**, **NTFS**, **FAT32**, and **exFAT**. When mounting a device, Unix needs to know the file system type to handle the device correctly.

    To specify the file system type when mounting, use the `-t` option with the `mount` command. For example, to mount a FAT32 formatted USB drive:

    bash
    Copy

```
sudo mount -t vfat /dev/sdb1 /mnt
```

12.

If you're unsure about the file system type, you can use the `blkid` command to display the file system type of all your devices:

bash
Copy

```
sudo blkid
```

13.

14. **Automatic Mounting**: If you want a device to be mounted automatically at boot, you can add it to the `/etc/fstab` file. This file contains information about file systems and how they should be mounted during startup. Each line in `/etc/fstab` defines a device, its mount point, the file system type, and mounting options.

    For example, to automatically mount `/dev/sda1` to `/mnt` at boot, you would add a line like this to `/etc/fstab`:

    bash
    Copy

```
/dev/sda1      /mnt      ext4      defaults      0      0
```

15.

After making changes to `/etc/fstab`, you can apply them without rebooting by running:

bash
Copy

```
sudo mount -a
```

16.

17. Unmounting Drives is equally important to ensure data integrity. When you're done using a device, you should unmount it before removing it physically to prevent data corruption. To unmount a device, use the `umount` command:

bash
Copy

```
sudo umount /mnt
```

18.

If the device is busy (i.e., files are still open on the device), the unmounting process will fail. You can use the `lsof` command to check which processes are using the device:

bash
Copy

```
sudo lsof /mnt
```

19.

To safely unmount a device even if it's busy, you can use the `-l` (lazy) option with `umount`, which will postpone the unmount operation until it's no longer in use:

bash

```
sudo umount -l /mnt
```

20.

21. **Network File Systems (NFS)** allow you to mount directories from remote machines onto your local filesystem. This is useful for sharing files between different systems in a network. To mount a remote NFS share, you can use the `mount` command with the `nfs` option:
bash

```
sudo mount -t nfs server:/shared/directory /mnt
```

22.

Here, `server` is the IP address or hostname of the remote machine, and `/shared/directory` is the directory you want to mount. Once mounted, the remote directory will appear as if it's part of your local filesystem, and you can access its files just like any other directory.

23. **Samba (SMB/CIFS)** is another protocol for sharing files between different operating systems (e.g., between Linux and Windows). To mount a Samba share, use the following command:
bash

```
sudo mount -t cifs //server/share /mnt -o
username=user,password=pass
```

24.

Replace `server` with the IP address or hostname of the Samba server, and `share` with the shared directory. The `-o` option allows you to specify the username and password for authentication.

25. **Automating NFS and Samba Mounting**: Just as with local drives, you can add network file systems to `/etc/fstab` for automatic mounting at boot. For NFS, you would add

a line like:

bash

Copy

```
server:/shared/directory    /mnt    nfs    defaults
0    0
```

26.

For Samba shares, the `/etc/fstab` entry would look like this:

pgsql

Copy

```
//server/share    /mnt    cifs
username=user,password=pass    0    0
```

27.

This ensures that network shares are mounted automatically when the system boots up.

28. **Mounting ISO Files**: An ISO file is a disk image, typically used for distributing operating system installation discs or software. To mount an ISO file, you can use the `mount` command with the `-o loop` option, which treats the ISO file as if it were a physical disk:

bash

Copy

```
sudo mount -o loop file.iso /mnt
```

29.

This allows you to access the contents of the ISO file, such as an installation CD or a compressed file system.

30. **File System Checking and Repair**: Sometimes, a file system may become corrupted, especially after an improper shutdown or hardware failure. Unix provides the **fsck** (file system check) utility to check and repair file systems. To check a file system, run:

bash

Copy

```
sudo fsck /dev/sda1
```

31.

The `fsck` command will scan the file system for errors and attempt to repair them. It's important to unmount the file system before running `fsck`, or run it in **single-user mode** if you're checking the root file system.

32. **In conclusion**, mounting and unmounting are fundamental concepts in Unix that allow you to manage storage devices and network shares effectively. By understanding how to mount and unmount devices, configure automatic mounts, and troubleshoot issues like busy devices or file system errors, you can manage storage with ease. Whether you're working with local hard drives, networked file systems, or virtual file systems, the ability to mount and unmount drives is essential for interacting with your system's storage. So, take the time to practice these commands, and soon you'll be navigating your drives like a pro! Happy mounting!

Mount Options are another important consideration when mounting drives. Mount options allow you to customize the way a file system is accessed and used. These options can control everything from read/write access to file system performance and behavior under certain conditions.

For example, if you want to mount a drive in **read-only** mode, you can use the `ro` (read-only) option:

bash
Copy
```
sudo mount -o ro /dev/sda1 /mnt
```
This ensures that the drive can be read but not modified. Conversely, to allow both reading and writing, you can use the `rw` (read/write) option:

bash
Copy
```
sudo mount -o rw /dev/sda1 /mnt
```
Other useful mount options include:

- **noatime**: Disables the recording of access times for files, which can improve performance on systems with frequent file access.

- **defaults**: Uses the default options for the file system, which typically includes read/ write access, automatic mounting at boot, and other common settings.

- **sync**: Ensures that all data written to the file system is flushed to disk immediately, which can be useful for ensuring data integrity but may slow down performance.

To mount a drive with multiple options, separate them with commas:

bash
Copy
```
sudo mount -o rw,noatime /dev/sda1 /mnt
```
Automounting with `autofs` is another feature you can use to automatically mount devices when they are accessed, and unmount them after they're no longer in use. This can help reduce the need for manually mounting drives or network shares, especially in environments with numerous removable storage devices.

The **`autofs`** service can automatically mount and unmount devices on demand. It's typically used for mounting network shares, CD-ROMs, or other devices that aren't always connected.

To set up `autofs`, you need to modify the `/etc/auto.master` file to specify the location of the device you want to automatically mount. For example, to mount an NFS share when it's accessed:

bash
Copy
```
/mnt/nfs    /etc/auto.nfs
```
Then, create a file named `/etc/auto.nfs` that defines the NFS share:

nginx
Copy
```
share -fstype=nfs server:/shared/directory
```
Once configured, `autofs` will automatically mount the NFS share when you try to access `/mnt/nfs`, and unmount it when it's no longer in use.

Filesystem Hierarchy Standard (FHS) is an important concept when it comes to understanding where mounted devices appear in the filesystem. The FHS defines standard directory locations in Unix systems, so you know where to expect certain types of data.

For instance:

- **/mnt**: This is the traditional location where temporary mounts (like external drives) are made.

- **/media**: This is where removable media, such as USB drives, CDs, or DVDs, are usually mounted automatically by the system.

- **/home**: This is typically where user files are stored, and it is often mounted separately to protect user data from system issues.

Knowing these conventions helps you manage mounting effectively and makes navigating your system more intuitive.

Mounting with LVM (Logical Volume Management) provides a flexible way to manage storage by abstracting the underlying physical devices and creating logical volumes that can be resized dynamically. With LVM, you can combine multiple physical volumes (e.g., hard drives) into a single volume group and then create logical volumes from that group.

To create an LVM-based mount, you first need to create a volume group and logical volume. For example, you can create a logical volume on a volume group:

```bash
sudo lvcreate -L 10G -n myvolume myvolume_group
```

After creating the logical volume, you can format it and mount it just like any other partition:

```bash
sudo mkfs.ext4 /dev/myvolume_group/myvolume
sudo mount /dev/myvolume_group/myvolume /mnt
```

LVM allows you to resize the logical volumes as needed without needing to reformat or repartition your disks, making it a powerful tool for dynamic storage management.

Troubleshooting Mount Issues can be tricky, especially if a drive doesn't mount automatically or if you run into errors during the mounting process. Here are a few common problems and solutions:

- **"Device is busy" error**: This usually happens if the device is in use by a process. You can check which processes are using the device with `lsof` or `fuser`:

  ```bash
  sudo lsof /mnt
  ```

- `sudo fuser /mnt`

-

  If a process is found, terminate it or close the files that are open on the device, then try mounting again.

- **Invalid file system type**: If you're getting an error saying the file system type is incorrect, double-check that you're using the correct type. You can run `blkid` to verify the file system type of the device, or use `mount` with the `-t` option to explicitly specify the file system type.

- **"No such device" error**: If you see this error, ensure the device is properly connected and recognized by your system. Use the `lsblk` or `fdisk -l` command to list all connected devices and verify that the device exists.

Unmounting Removable Devices is important to ensure that files are written and no processes are left open before physically removing the device. Always unmount USB drives, external hard drives, or network shares before disconnecting them. Failing to do so can result in data corruption.

To unmount a device, use the `umount` command with the device or the mount point:

```bash
Copy
sudo umount /mnt
```

If you're unsure of the device's mount point, you can use `lsblk` to list the mounted devices and their respective mount points.

In conclusion, mounting and unmounting are fundamental tasks that form the backbone of file system management in Unix. From mounting local hard drives and network shares to configuring automatic mounting with `fstab` or `autofs`, mastering the art of mounting ensures that you can seamlessly manage your system's storage. With the right tools and techniques, you can easily control access to your drives, optimize your file system's performance, and ensure data integrity. As you continue to explore and manage your Unix system, mounting and unmounting will become second nature—just another powerful tool in your Unix toolkit. Happy mounting!

Chapter 22: File Systems Unplugged: A Deep Dive into the Storage Matrix

1. When it comes to managing data on a Unix system, understanding **file systems** is key to unlocking the full potential of your storage devices. Just as a city's road network determines how efficiently traffic flows, the file system governs how data is organized, accessed, and stored. In this chapter, we're going to take a deep dive into the **storage matrix**, exploring the different types of file systems, their features, and how they impact your system's performance, scalability, and data integrity. Whether you're dealing with local hard drives, network storage, or specialized file systems for cloud and virtual environments, this knowledge will help you make informed decisions when configuring and optimizing your Unix system.

2. **What is a File System?** A file system is the method by which files are named, stored, and retrieved on a storage device. It defines the structure in which files are organized and manages the mapping between the files' logical names and their physical locations on the storage medium. Without a file system, data would be an incoherent blob of bytes, impossible to retrieve or organize.
There are several types of file systems available in Unix, each with its own strengths and weaknesses. Some file systems are optimized for performance, while others are designed for robustness or specific use cases. The choice of file system can significantly impact how your system handles data and interacts with storage devices.

3. **Common Unix File Systems**: Let's start by exploring the most commonly used file systems in Unix-based systems. Each file system type has unique features, and the right choice depends on your system's needs.

   o **ext4 (Fourth Extended File System)**: This is the default file system on many Linux distributions, including Ubuntu. It's widely used due to its performance, reliability, and support for large files and volumes. `ext4` supports journaling, which helps prevent data corruption during power outages or system crashes. It also features excellent file system consistency checks and offers a good balance between speed and robustness.

   o **xfs**: XFS is another high-performance file system designed for handling large files and large file systems. It's particularly well-suited for high-performance computing environments, such as databases and large storage systems. XFS supports **dynamic inode allocation**, which improves performance for systems with many files, and it also features built-in **data deduplication** for better storage efficiency.

   o **btrfs (B-tree File System)**: Btrfs is a modern file system that supports features like snapshots, compression, and integrated RAID functionality. It's designed to be highly flexible and scalable, offering advanced features for managing large storage arrays and improving system resilience. Btrfs can take **read-only snapshots** of your file system, allowing you to easily roll back to a previous state if something goes wrong.

4. **The ext3 File System**: Before `ext4`, `ext3` was the default file system for many Linux systems. Although `ext3` is still supported, it's now considered outdated. Like `ext4`, `ext3` supports journaling, which allows it to recover quickly after a crash. However, `ext3` lacks many of the performance optimizations and features found in `ext4`, such as support for large files and volumes. If you're working with an older system, you may encounter `ext3` but should consider migrating to `ext4` for better performance.

5. **FAT and NTFS File Systems**: While Unix systems typically use native file systems like `ext4` or `xfs`, you may need to interact with **FAT** (File Allocation Table) or **NTFS** (New Technology File System) file systems, especially when sharing files between Unix and Windows machines.

   o **FAT32** is a simple file system commonly used for external drives and USB flash drives. It's supported by nearly every operating system, including Unix, Windows, and macOS. However, `FAT32` has limitations, such as a maximum file size of 4GB and lack of journaling, making it less suitable for larger or more demanding systems.

   o **NTFS**, the default file system on Windows, is supported on Linux through third-party drivers, such as **ntfs-3g**. NTFS is known for its robustness, support for large files, and file system journaling. It's widely used for multi-OS environments where files need to be shared between Windows and Unix systems.

6. **File System Hierarchy**: Every file system is structured in a way that defines how files and directories are organized. In Unix-based systems, the root directory (`/`) is the top-level directory of the file system. Under the root directory, you'll find other important directories like `/home`, `/usr`, and `/var`, each with specific purposes.

   o   **/home** is where user directories are stored.

   o   **/usr** contains essential system programs and libraries.

   o   **/var** holds variable files like logs and spool files.

7. File systems in Unix follow the **Filesystem Hierarchy Standard (FHS)**, which defines the directory structure and ensures consistency across different Unix-like systems. Understanding this structure is key when managing your file system and organizing data efficiently.

8. **Mounting File Systems**: To interact with a storage device, it must be **mounted** to a directory in the file system. Mounting a device makes it accessible through the directory hierarchy, allowing you to read from and write to it. For example, if you want to mount a USB drive, you would typically use the `mount` command to attach it to a directory, such as `/mnt/usb`. Once mounted, the contents of the USB drive are accessible through the `/mnt/usb` directory.
Example of mounting a device:
bash
Copy

```
sudo mount /dev/sdb1 /mnt/usb
```

9.

   The device `/dev/sdb1` is mounted to the `/mnt/usb` directory, allowing you to access the files on the USB drive. Unmounting the drive when you're done is equally important to prevent data loss.

10. **Journaling File Systems**: A file system's **journaling** feature is one of the most important aspects in maintaining file system integrity. When a file system is journaled, it keeps a log (or journal) of changes that will be made to the file system. In the event of a crash or power failure, the system can use this log to recover or rollback changes and prevent corruption. Both `ext4` and `xfs` support journaling, making them resilient to system crashes and ensuring data integrity.

11. **Advanced File System Features**:

   o **Snapshots**: Some file systems, like `btrfs`, support **snapshots**, which allow you to capture the state of the file system at a specific point in time. Snapshots are useful for backups, as they enable you to preserve the state of the system without needing to take the file system offline.

   o **Compression**: File systems like `btrfs` and `zfs` also support **compression**, allowing data to be stored in a smaller size, reducing storage requirements. Compression can be particularly useful on systems with limited disk space or when working with large datasets.

   o **Deduplication**: File systems like `zfs` and `btrfs` support **deduplication**, which automatically identifies and eliminates duplicate files, saving disk space.

12. **Understanding Disk Partitions and Logical Volumes**: File systems don't exist in a vacuum; they are applied to specific areas on a disk, known as **partitions**. Partitions are like separate sections on a physical disk where file systems can reside.

   o **Primary Partitions** are the main partitions on a hard drive.

   o **Logical Partitions** are created within an extended partition, allowing you to create more than four partitions.

13. Additionally, **Logical Volume Management (LVM)** allows you to manage disk space more flexibly by abstracting physical devices into logical volumes that can be resized, combined, or split as needed.

14. **Network File Systems (NFS and SMB)**: For distributed systems, you'll often need to access files across a network. **Network File Systems (NFS)** and **Server Message Block (SMB)** are commonly used protocols for sharing files over a network.

   o **NFS** is commonly used in Unix environments to mount remote file systems over a network, allowing for easy access to shared directories.

   o **SMB** (commonly used in Windows) allows Unix systems to access shared folders on Windows machines. Tools like **Samba** enable Unix systems to share files with Windows systems using the SMB protocol.

15. **File System Maintenance**: File systems require regular maintenance to ensure they continue to function smoothly and efficiently. Key maintenance tasks include:

   o **Checking the file system**: Use `fsck` to check and repair file system errors:
   bash
   Copy

```
sudo fsck /dev/sda1
```

- o

  - o **Optimizing disk space**: Use tools like `du` and `df` to monitor disk usage and free up space by removing unnecessary files or cleaning up temporary directories.

16. **In conclusion**, understanding file systems is a vital skill for managing Unix systems, whether you're handling local disks, network file systems, or advanced storage solutions. By knowing the ins and outs of file system types, mounting, file system features, and maintenance, you can ensure your system's data is organized, secure, and performing at its best. Whether you're dealing with the reliable `ext4` file system or the flexible `btrfs`, having a deep understanding of the storage matrix will allow you to tailor your storage solutions to meet your specific needs. Happy diving into the world of file systems!

Understanding File System Performance is another key aspect of working with different file systems. Different file systems have varying performance characteristics, and the choice of file system can greatly influence how quickly data is read from or written to the storage device. Factors such as **I/O performance**, **disk space utilization**, and **metadata overhead** can all impact how well a file system performs under different workloads.

- **ext4** is known for being well-balanced in terms of both read and write performance, making it an excellent choice for general-purpose use. However, its performance might not be the best for systems handling large databases or heavy I/O workloads.

- **xfs** excels in handling large files and high-performance workloads, making it a preferred choice for servers and high-throughput systems. It's particularly efficient in dealing with parallel I/O operations and large databases.

- **btrfs** offers advanced features like snapshots and compression, but its performance may suffer when it comes to high-speed workloads, particularly in write-heavy scenarios. However, its ability to handle dynamic resizing and easy snapshot creation makes it ideal for environments that require frequent backups or data versioning.

When choosing a file system, consider your system's workload and the types of data you're managing. Performance tuning and optimization techniques can help you maximize the benefits of your chosen file system.

File System Encryption is another layer of protection you can apply to safeguard sensitive data. **Encrypting a file system** ensures that data stored on the drive remains protected, even if the physical device is lost or stolen. Various file systems and tools provide encryption options, allowing you to choose between full-disk encryption or encrypting individual files and directories.

- **LUKS** (Linux Unified Key Setup) is a popular tool for encrypting entire disk partitions. It provides strong encryption standards and is widely supported across different Linux distributions.

- **ecryptfs** is a stackable file system that can be used to encrypt individual directories or files. It works transparently, meaning that files are encrypted as they're written and decrypted as they're read.

When using file system encryption, keep your encryption keys secure, as they are the only way to access your encrypted data. Encryption ensures confidentiality but may add some overhead to performance, so it's essential to weigh the trade-offs based on your security needs.

Data Integrity and Reliability: In any file system, ensuring data integrity is critical to preventing corruption and loss of data. Some file systems, like **ZFS** and **btrfs**, offer built-in checksums for all data and metadata, providing **self-healing** capabilities. This means that if a data block gets corrupted, the system can automatically detect the error and attempt to correct it using redundant or backup data. This feature is particularly useful for systems with high availability requirements and those with large amounts of critical data.

- **ZFS** is known for its ability to detect and repair data corruption automatically. ZFS combines features of both file systems and volume managers, making it an excellent choice for large-scale, high-reliability systems.

- **btrfs** also offers checksumming for data integrity, along with features like snapshotting, which makes it a strong contender for both personal and enterprise-level systems where data integrity is paramount.

Understanding how your file system handles data integrity can help you make better decisions when configuring storage and backups for your system.

Managing Disk Usage with File Systems involves understanding how your chosen file system utilizes disk space. Some file systems, like **ext4** and **xfs**, are quite efficient at managing space on a disk, allocating blocks and inodes as needed. However, file systems can experience **fragmentation** over time, particularly on systems that frequently write and delete large files.

- **Fragmentation** occurs when data is not stored contiguously on the disk, leading to slower read and write operations as the system has to seek out scattered blocks.

- While **ext4** has improved handling of fragmentation over its predecessors, it can still become fragmented in high-write environments. **xfs** and **btrfs**, on the other hand, handle fragmentation more efficiently, but regular defragmentation might be necessary for systems under heavy use.

To monitor disk usage and prevent fragmentation, you can use tools like `df`, `du`, and `fsck` to analyze disk space and run checks on your file systems.

File System Recovery: In the event of corruption or data loss, the ability to recover data from a file system can be crucial. Many Unix-based file systems offer tools for file system recovery, though the effectiveness of these tools depends on the type of corruption and the file system used.

- **ext4**: If an ext4 file system becomes corrupted, you can use **fsck** to attempt repairs. **fsck.ext4** scans the file system for errors and attempts to fix them. However, depending on the severity of the corruption, some data may be lost in the recovery process.

- **xfs**: XFS includes the **xfs_repair** tool for file system recovery. It's specifically designed to handle XFS file systems and can fix issues such as damaged superblocks and corrupted metadata.

- **btrfs**: Btrfs includes advanced tools for recovery, such as **btrfs check** and **btrfs restore**, which can attempt to recover data even if the file system becomes corrupt. It's particularly useful for environments where snapshots are taken regularly, as you can roll back to a previous known-good state.

Always ensure that you have a reliable backup strategy in place to protect against data loss, as file system recovery tools may not always be able to recover everything.

The Role of File System in Virtualization: In virtualized environments, managing storage efficiently is crucial for ensuring performance and scalability. Virtualization technologies like **Docker** and **VMware** rely heavily on file systems to manage virtual disk images, container data, and persistent storage.

- **Docker** uses a union file system (like **aufs**, **overlay2**, or **btrfs**) to manage container images. This file system allows multiple layers of a container to be stacked on top of each other, creating a lightweight and efficient method for managing virtualized application environments.

- **VMware** and other hypervisors use specialized virtual file systems (such as **VMFS** or **vmdk**) for managing virtual machines' storage. These file systems are optimized for high-performance and virtual disk management, allowing multiple virtual machines to share physical disk resources while maintaining isolation.

When working with virtualization, understanding how your file system handles virtual disk management, snapshots, and performance can help ensure a smooth, efficient, and scalable deployment.

In conclusion, file systems are the unsung heroes of Unix-based systems, quietly managing and organizing data in ways that make our daily computing tasks possible. By understanding the different types of file systems, their features, and their limitations, you can make informed decisions about which file system is best suited for your needs. Whether you're dealing with performance optimization, ensuring data integrity, managing disk space, or recovering from data loss, a deep understanding of file systems will empower you to manage your system more efficiently. So dive deep into the storage matrix, experiment with different file systems, and make your Unix environment work for you. Happy exploring the world of file systems!

Chapter 23: The Bash Shell: Not Just for Turtles

1. If you've ever heard of the **Bash shell**, you might have imagined a tiny turtle slowly waddling across a beach while pondering deep questions about life and technology. Well, you're not entirely wrong—after all, the name **Bash** stands for **Bourne Again SHell** (a clever play on the original Bourne shell). However, the Bash shell is far more than a casual stroll in the sand. In fact, it's one of the most powerful and versatile tools in the Unix arsenal. In this chapter, we'll dive into the world of the **Bash shell**, exploring its capabilities, features, and the magical ways it makes working with your system easier, faster, and more efficient. Whether you're a beginner or an experienced user, mastering Bash is a key part of becoming a Unix wizard. Let's unlock the shell's true potential.

2. **What is Bash?** At its core, **Bash** is a command-line interface (CLI) that allows you to interact with your system by typing commands, rather than relying on a graphical user interface (GUI). While the GUI might provide buttons and menus, the Bash shell gives you direct access to the system's underlying functionality through commands, scripts, and text-based input. It allows you to execute programs, manage files, manipulate system settings, and automate tasks—all from the comfort of a terminal window.
The Bash shell is **sh**-compatible (from the Bourne shell), meaning it supports many of the same commands and syntax, while also introducing powerful new features. It's widely used as the default shell on most Linux and macOS systems, and it can even be installed on Windows through **Windows Subsystem for Linux** (WSL).

3. **The Power of the Command Prompt**: When you open a terminal in a Unix-based system, you're greeted by the **command prompt** (also known as the **shell prompt**). This is where you can type commands to execute them. For example, you might see something like:

```ruby
```
Copy

```
user@hostname:~$
```

4.

The prompt shows your current **username**, the **hostname** of the system, and your **current directory** (~ for the home directory). You can type commands at the prompt to interact with your system. For example:

```bash
```
Copy

5.
```
ls
```

The `ls` command lists the files and directories in the current directory. The shell waits for you to type a command, executes it, and then returns the output to the prompt.

6. **Command History**: One of the best features of the Bash shell is its ability to remember the commands you've previously typed. This is thanks to **command history**, which allows you to scroll through the commands you've entered in the past and quickly reuse them.

You can access your command history by pressing the **up arrow** to scroll backward and the **down arrow** to scroll forward. If you want to see a list of previously executed commands, simply type:

bash
Copy

7.
```
history
```

This will display a numbered list of recent commands. You can also execute a command from history by referencing its number:

bash
Copy

8.
```
!5
```

This will execute the fifth command in your history list.

9. **Wildcards and Globbing**: Bash allows you to use **wildcards** (also known as **globbing**) to match files and directories. Wildcards are shorthand symbols that allow you to match one or more characters in filenames, making it easy to work with large numbers of files.

- `*` matches any number of characters:
  bash
  Copy

```bash
ls *.txt
```

o

This will list all files in the current directory with the `.txt` extension.

o **?** matches a single character:
```bash
Copy
```

```bash
ls file?.txt
```

o

This will match files like `file1.txt`, `file2.txt`, etc.

o **[ ]** matches a specific range or set of characters:
```bash
Copy
```

```bash
ls file[1-3].txt
```

o

This will match `file1.txt`, `file2.txt`, and `file3.txt`.

10. Wildcards save you time and keystrokes when dealing with large sets of files.

11. Pipes and Redirection: Bash allows you to redirect input and output between commands using **pipes** (|) and **redirection operators** (>, <). This is one of the most powerful aspects of the shell, as it allows you to chain commands together and manipulate data streams.

o **Pipes** (|) take the output of one command and pass it as input to another:
```bash
Copy
```

```
ls | grep "file"
```

-

    This command lists all files and then filters the results to show only files that contain the word "file."

- **Redirection (>, <)** allows you to send output to a file or read input from a file:
  bash
  Copy

```
echo "Hello, World!" > hello.txt
```

-

    This command writes "Hello, World!" to a file called `hello.txt`. The `>` operator overwrites the file, while `>>` appends to it.

- **Input redirection** allows you to feed a file's contents into a command:
  bash
  Copy

```
cat < hello.txt
```

-

12. The ability to pipe and redirect data makes Bash an incredibly powerful tool for managing and processing data on the fly.

13. **Variables and Environment Variables**: Bash allows you to create **variables** to store data and reuse it throughout your scripts or terminal sessions. You can create variables in the shell by simply assigning a value:
bash
Copy

```
my_variable="Hello, World!"
```

14. `echo $my_variable`
15.

This will output `Hello, World!`. Variables are useful for storing values like file paths, system settings, or user input.

Environment variables are special variables that affect the behavior of processes and programs on the system. Common environment variables include `$HOME` (the user's home directory), `$PATH` (the directories the shell searches for commands), and `$USER` (the current user's name). You can list all environment variables by typing:

bash
Copy

```
printenv
```

16.

17. **Scripting with Bash**: One of the most powerful features of Bash is its ability to automate tasks using **shell scripts**. A shell script is a simple text file containing a sequence of commands that can be executed all at once. Bash scripts are often used for automating repetitive tasks, system administration, or managing files.

A simple Bash script might look like this:

bash
Copy

```
#!/bin/bash
```

18. `echo "Hello, World!"`
19.

The first line (`#!/bin/bash`) is called the **shebang** and tells the system to execute the script with the Bash shell. After making the script executable (`chmod +x script.sh`), you can run it by typing:

bash
Copy

```
./script.sh
```

20.

Scripts can include loops, conditionals, functions, and more. For example, a script to back up a directory might look like:

bash
Copy

```
#!/bin/bash
```
21. `tar -czf backup.tar.gz /home/user/data`

22.

With Bash scripting, you can automate nearly any task on your Unix system, saving time and reducing human error.

23. Conditionals and Loops: Bash supports traditional programming constructs such as **if-else** statements and **for/while loops**. These constructs allow you to perform conditional execution and repeat commands.

Example of a **simple if-else** statement:

bash
Copy

```
if [ -f file.txt ]; then
```
24.   `echo "File exists"`
25. `else`
26.   `echo "File does not exist"`
27. `fi`
28.

Example of a **for loop**:

bash
Copy

```
for i in {1..5}; do
```
29.   `echo "Number $i"`
30. `done`

31.

This loop prints the numbers 1 through 5. Bash loops are a great way to iterate over a range of items, such as files or directories, and perform actions on each.

32. **Debugging Bash Scripts**: As with any programming language, debugging is an essential part of the process. Fortunately, Bash provides a variety of tools to help with debugging.

- ○ You can enable **debugging mode** by adding the **-x** option to your script or using **set -x** inside the script:

  ```bash
  Copy
  ```

  ```
  set -x
  ```

- ○

- ○ If you want the script to stop execution when an error occurs, use the **set -e** option:

  ```bash
  Copy
  ```

  ```
  set -e
  ```

- ○

33. These options help trace the script's execution and catch errors early.

34. **In conclusion**, the Bash shell is far more than just a command-line interface—it's a powerful tool for interacting with your system, automating tasks, and managing your environment. Whether you're navigating the filesystem, running commands, creating scripts, or configuring your environment, mastering Bash is an essential skill for anyone using a Unix-based system. With the knowledge and techniques covered in this chapter, you now have the tools to take full advantage of Bash's capabilities, helping you work more efficiently and effectively. Happy shell scripting!

Bash Functions and Parameter Expansion are two advanced features that allow you to write cleaner, more efficient scripts. **Functions** in Bash allow you to bundle commands together and reuse them. You can pass **arguments** to functions, making your scripts more modular and flexible. Here's an example of a Bash function:

```bash
Copy
greet_user() {
    echo "Hello, $1!"
}

greet_user "Alice"
```
In this example, the function `greet_user` takes one parameter, `$1`, and prints a greeting. You can pass `"Alice"` as the argument to the function, and the output will be `Hello, Alice!`.

Parameter expansion in Bash allows you to manipulate variables in powerful ways. For example, you can extract substrings, perform case transformations, or replace parts of a string. Here are a few examples:

- Extract a substring:
  ```bash
  Copy
  string="Hello, World!"
  ```
- `echo ${string:7:5}`
-

  This will output `World`, as it extracts 5 characters starting from position 7.
- Replace part of a string:
  ```bash
  Copy
  string="Hello, World!"
  ```
- `echo ${string/World/Unix}`
-

  This will output `Hello, Unix!`, as it replaces `World` with `Unix`.

Job Control in Bash allows you to manage background and foreground processes. Sometimes, you may want to run a command in the background so you can continue working on other tasks in the terminal. You can do this by appending an **ampersand (&)** to the end of the command:

```bash
```
Copy
```bash
sleep 30 &
```

This will run the `sleep 30` command in the background, allowing you to run other commands without waiting for `sleep` to finish. You can check the background jobs by typing `jobs`:

```bash
```
Copy
```bash
jobs
```

If you want to bring a background job to the foreground, you can use the `fg` command, followed by the job number:

```bash
```
Copy
```bash
fg %1
```

Job control is helpful for multitasking within a single terminal session.

Aliases and Functions for Efficiency are fantastic for making repetitive tasks easier and faster. **Aliases** in Bash allow you to create shortcuts for long or complex commands. For example, you could create an alias to list all files, including hidden files:

```bash
```
Copy
```bash
alias ll='ls -la'
```

Now, every time you type `ll`, it will execute `ls -la`. Aliases are especially helpful for custom commands you use frequently.

Similarly, you can create more complex **functions** for tasks you often perform. For instance, you might have a function to back up a directory:

```bash
```
Copy
```bash
backup() {
    tar -czf "$1_backup.tar.gz" "$1"
}
```

This function takes a directory name as an argument and creates a compressed backup of it. You can call the function with:

```bash
```
Copy
```bash
backup /home/user/data
```

Aliases and functions can make your Bash environment much more efficient and tailored to your workflow.

Bash Regular Expressions are an incredibly powerful feature for pattern matching. In Bash, you can use regular expressions (regex) with commands like `grep`, `sed`, and `awk` to search and manipulate text data. For example, you can use `grep` to find lines in a file that match a specific pattern:

```bash
grep '^error' logfile.txt
```

This command will match all lines in `logfile.txt` that start with the word "error". Regular expressions allow you to do complex pattern matching with just a few characters, such as `*`, `+`, `?`, and `[ ]`.

- `^` matches the beginning of a line.

- `$` matches the end of a line.

- `.*` matches any number of characters.

Regular expressions are an essential tool for text processing in Bash, enabling you to work with large datasets or logs quickly and effectively.

Bash Job Control allows you to manage processes more efficiently, especially when you need to run commands in the background or bring them to the foreground. Unix-based systems often require running multiple tasks simultaneously, and Bash makes it easy to manage these tasks using job control features. One of the most common tasks is running a process in the **background**, so it doesn't block your terminal session. You can do this by appending `&` to the end of a command:

```bash
long_running_task &
```

This command runs `long_running_task` in the background, allowing you to continue working in the terminal. To see a list of all running jobs, use the `jobs` command:

```bash
jobs
```

If you want to bring a background job back to the foreground, use the `fg` command, followed by the job number:

```bash
fg %1
```

This will bring the first job in the list to the foreground. Similarly, you can pause jobs with `Ctrl+Z` and resume them in the background with `bg`.

Working with Processes in Bash: Bash allows you to manage processes directly from the terminal, making it easy to monitor and control your system's resource usage. The `ps` command shows information about running processes, such as their process ID (PID), the user running the process, and the resource usage. To see a list of all running processes, use:

```bash
ps aux
```

- `ps` shows processes.

- `a` lists processes for all users.

- `u` adds user-oriented output.

- `x` shows processes that are not attached to a terminal.

If you want to kill a process, you can use the `kill` command followed by the process ID (PID):

```bash
kill <PID>
```

If a process refuses to terminate, you can force it to quit by using `kill -9`:

```bash
kill -9 <PID>
```

Bash makes it easy to interact with and manage your system's running processes, giving you control over how resources are allocated and how long tasks run.

Using Bash for System Administration: Bash is not just for interacting with files or writing scripts—it is a powerful tool for system administration. From creating and managing users to configuring system settings, Bash is integral to managing and automating system tasks. For example, you can add a new user with the `useradd` command:

```bash
sudo useradd newuser
sudo passwd newuser
```

This creates a new user and sets their password. You can also delete users with `userdel`:

```bash
```

```
sudo userdel newuser
```
Bash also helps with managing system services. For example, you can restart a service with `systemctl`:

```bash
```
Copy
```
sudo systemctl restart apache2
```
This command will restart the Apache web server, a crucial tool for web server management. Bash allows system administrators to automate and script such tasks to save time and reduce manual errors.

Bash for Text Processing: Bash is a master at handling and manipulating text files, which makes it invaluable for processing logs, configuration files, and other forms of textual data. You can use tools like **grep**, **sed**, and **awk** to search, replace, and format text in files.

- **grep** is used to search for patterns in files. For example, to search for the word "error" in a log file:
  ```bash
  ```
  Copy

  ```
  grep "error" logfile.txt
  ```

-

- **sed** (stream editor) is a powerful tool for editing text within files. For instance, to replace all occurrences of "old" with "new" in a file:
  ```bash
  ```
  Copy

  ```
  sed -i 's/old/new/g' file.txt
  ```

-

- **awk** is another text-processing powerhouse that allows you to split and manipulate text based on patterns. For example, to print the first column from a CSV file:
  ```bash
  ```
  Copy

```
awk -F, '{print $1}' file.csv
```

•

These tools are highly flexible and can be combined to create advanced text-processing scripts.

Advanced Bash Scripting: As you get more comfortable with Bash, you can create more advanced scripts to automate complex tasks. Bash supports a variety of features, such as **loops**, **conditionals**, **arrays**, and **functions**, that allow you to build robust, modular scripts.

- **Arrays** allow you to store and process lists of data. For example:
  bash
  Copy

```
fruits=("apple" "banana" "cherry")
```
- ```
  for fruit in "${fruits[@]}"; do
  ```
- ```
      echo $fruit
  ```
- ```
  done
  ```
-

- **Functions** help organize your code and allow you to reuse blocks of commands. Here's an example:
  bash
  Copy

```
greet_user() {
```
- ```
      echo "Hello, $1!"
  ```
- ```
  }
  ```
- ```
  greet_user "Alice"
  ```
-

- **Conditionals** and **loops** let you control the flow of execution in your script. For example, an **if-else** statement can be used to check conditions:
  bash
  Copy

```bash
if [ -f "file.txt" ]; then
```
- ```bash
      echo "File exists!"
  ```
- ```bash
  else
  ```
- ```bash
      echo "File not found."
  ```
- ```bash
  fi
  ```
-

These features make Bash a powerful tool for writing automation scripts, system maintenance tasks, and handling repetitive processes efficiently.

Bash for Networking: Bash is also a versatile tool for managing and interacting with network resources. Whether you're checking for network connectivity or managing remote servers, Bash commands and scripts are essential.

- To check if a remote server is up and running, you can use **ping**:
  bash
  Copy

```bash
ping -c 4 example.com
```

-

- **ssh** allows you to remotely log into another system, which is essential for system administrators. For example:
  bash
  Copy

```bash
ssh user@remote-server
```

-

- You can also use **scp** (Secure Copy Protocol) to transfer files between systems securely:
  bash
  Copy

```
scp file.txt user@remote-server:/path/to/destination
```

-

Networking tasks such as checking connectivity, transferring files, and remote system management are simple and quick with Bash.

Bash Debugging Tools: When writing more complex Bash scripts, debugging becomes an important part of the process. Fortunately, Bash provides several tools to help with debugging:

- Use **set -x** to trace each command executed within the script. This can help you identify where errors occur:
  bash
  Copy

  ```
  set -x
  ```

-

- Use **set -e** to make the script exit immediately if any command fails. This ensures that errors are caught early:
  bash
  Copy

  ```
  set -e
  ```

-

- You can also add **echo** statements at strategic points in your script to display the values of variables or the output of commands.

Debugging in Bash is essential for ensuring that scripts run smoothly, especially when they involve complex logic or large datasets.

In conclusion, the **Bash shell** is not just for beginners or turtles; it's an incredibly powerful tool that serves as the backbone of Unix-based systems. From managing files and automating tasks to handling system administration and networking, mastering Bash will dramatically increase your efficiency and control over your system. Whether you're writing simple one-liners or creating sophisticated scripts, Bash is the essential tool you'll use every day. So, embrace the shell, unleash its full potential, and enjoy the flexibility and power it brings to your Unix experience. Happy scripting!

Chapter 24: Going Beyond Bash: Advanced Shells for the Adventurous

1. **Bash** is undoubtedly the most popular shell for Unix-based systems, and for good reason. It's powerful, versatile, and comes pre-installed on most systems. However, **Bash** is just one of many shells available for interacting with the system. If you're ready to push your shell skills further, there are several other advanced shells that offer unique features, improved performance, and additional functionalities for those who crave something more than the standard Bash experience. In this chapter, we'll explore some of these **advanced shells**, examining their distinctive features, advantages, and why they might appeal to the adventurous Unix user.

2. **Zsh (Z Shell)**: One of the most popular alternatives to Bash is **Zsh** (Z Shell). Zsh is known for its impressive feature set, including enhanced tab completion, better history management, and superior scripting capabilities. It offers a more user-friendly experience with better **auto-completion**, **globbing**, and **pattern matching**.

   One of Zsh's standout features is its **interactive features**. For example, Zsh has **advanced tab completion**, which can complete not just file names but also command options, function names, and more. If you type a command and press `Tab`, Zsh will offer suggestions for completing the command based on context.

   Zsh also allows you to **customize the prompt** in more interesting ways than Bash. With Zsh, you can easily add information about the current git branch, the status of your last command, or your system's performance metrics right into the prompt.

   To install Zsh:

   ```bash
   ```
   Copy

   ```
   sudo apt install zsh
   ```

3.

   After installation, you can change your default shell to Zsh using:

   ```bash
   ```
   Copy

   ```
   chsh -s $(which zsh)
   ```

4.

Zsh is often the preferred choice for users who want a more feature-rich interactive shell experience and for those who appreciate a highly customizable environment.

5. Fish (Friendly Interactive Shell): If you're looking for a shell that combines the ease of use with powerful features, **Fish** is an excellent choice. Fish is designed to be simple and user-friendly, with **automatic suggestions**, **syntax highlighting**, and **easy-to-read error messages**.

Fish's standout feature is its **autosuggestions**. As you type, Fish will suggest commands based on your command history or common patterns, making it much faster to execute common tasks. Fish also provides **syntax highlighting**, so if you make a typo or enter a command incorrectly, it will be highlighted in color, making it easy to spot errors in real-time.

Unlike Zsh and Bash, Fish doesn't rely on **bashrc** or **zshrc** files for customization. Instead, it uses a dedicated configuration file that is more user-friendly, with commands written in Fish's own scripting language.

To install Fish:

bash
Copy

```
sudo apt install fish
```

6.

To change your default shell to Fish:

bash
Copy

```
chsh -s $(which fish)
```

7.

Fish is a great shell for beginners who want powerful features out of the box without the need for heavy configuration or scripting knowledge.

8. Tcsh (TENEX C Shell): Tcsh is a variant of the original **C shell (csh)** and is known for its **command-line editing** and **file name completion** features. Tcsh offers a **C-like syntax**, which may appeal to users who are familiar with programming languages like C or Java. While it is not as widely used as Zsh or Bash, it has a loyal user base that appreciates its syntax and advanced features.

Some of Tcsh's features include **command history**, **customizable prompts**, and the ability to **work with a variety of wildcard characters** for file completion. It also includes a unique feature called **aliasing**, which allows you to define new commands or shortcuts for frequent tasks.

To install Tcsh:

bash
Copy

```
sudo apt install tcsh
```

9.

Tcsh is a good choice for users who prefer the C shell's syntax and want a customizable, efficient interactive shell experience.

10. **Ksh (KornShell)**: **Ksh** is an advanced shell that combines the features of the Bourne shell (`sh`) with additional features for scripting, making it a powerful tool for users who need to write complex scripts. Ksh offers better performance for large-scale scripts than some other shells, and its scripting features make it ideal for system administrators.

Ksh has built-in support for **command history**, **job control**, **pattern matching**, and **scripting functions**. One of its most notable features is its **brace expansion** and **command substitution**, which allow for complex operations to be done more easily. For example, Ksh provides a shorthand for creating lists of files or iterating over a set of items.

To install Ksh:

bash
Copy

```
sudo apt install ksh
```

11.

Ksh is best suited for users who prefer a scripting environment that's more consistent with traditional Unix shells but still offers advanced features for automation and scripting.

12. **Dash (Debian Almquist Shell)**: If you need a **lightweight shell** that's optimized for performance and used primarily for scripting, **Dash** is an excellent choice. Dash is often the default shell for **system scripts** on Debian-based distributions, including Ubuntu. It's designed to be **fast** and **minimalistic**, so if you're working on scripts where performance is critical, Dash might be the shell for you.

Dash is a POSIX-compliant shell, which means it sticks closely to the specifications of the **POSIX shell** standard. While it may not offer as many interactive features as Zsh or Fish, Dash's focus is on executing scripts quickly and efficiently, making it ideal for system-level tasks.

Dash is usually pre-installed on many systems, but you can switch to it if you prefer:

bash
Copy

```
sudo chsh -s /bin/dash
```

13.

Dash is a great choice for scripting, especially if you need to optimize for speed and compatibility with POSIX standards.

14. **Sh (Bourne Shell)**: The **Bourne shell (sh)** is the oldest and most basic Unix shell. While it doesn't have many of the features of more modern shells like Bash or Zsh, it's still commonly used for system scripts due to its **POSIX compliance** and simplicity. Most of the basic shell scripting techniques can be accomplished in `sh`, but modern features like interactive command completion, advanced tab expansion, and rich syntax are not available.

Despite its simplicity, **sh** remains an essential tool for writing scripts that need to run across different Unix-like systems, as it has very few dependencies.

15. **Advanced Shell Customization**: Many of these advanced shells provide powerful customization options, allowing you to tailor your environment to suit your needs. Whether it's tweaking your prompt with Zsh, adding aliases in Fish, or adjusting the file completion rules in Tcsh, customizing your shell environment can dramatically increase your productivity.

For example, in **Zsh**, you can change your prompt to display the current directory and git branch by editing your `.zshrc` file:

bash
Copy

```
PROMPT='%~ %(!.#.>)'   # Displays the current directory
and a prompt that changes based on user privileges.
```

16.

Similarly, Fish makes it easy to customize the shell environment by modifying its configuration file (`~/.config/fish/config.fish`). You can set environment variables, change prompt styles, and more, all without writing complex configuration scripts.

Exploring the advanced features of each shell and experimenting with different customizations can help you create an efficient and personalized terminal environment.

17. **Choosing the Right Shell**: Each of the shells we've discussed has its own set of strengths, and choosing the right shell often depends on your specific needs and preferences. Here are some guidelines to help you choose:

    o   Choose **Zsh** if you want a feature-rich shell with powerful tab completion, customization, and advanced scripting support.

    o   Opt for **Fish** if you prefer an easy-to-use, interactive shell with auto-suggestions and syntax highlighting, perfect for beginners and those who want a modern shell experience.

    o   **Tcsh** is best for those who prefer C-like syntax or are coming from a C programming background.

    o   **Ksh** is ideal for users who need a powerful, POSIX-compliant scripting shell for complex tasks and high-performance scripts.

    o   **Dash** is perfect for system scripts where speed and minimal resource usage are crucial.

    o   Stick with **sh** if you need simplicity and POSIX compliance across different systems.

18. **In conclusion**, Bash is an excellent shell, but there's a whole world of other shells out there to explore. From Zsh's customizability and Fish's user-friendly features to the speed of Dash and the power of Ksh, these advanced shells can help you work smarter, faster, and more efficiently. Whether you're looking to optimize your interactive experience or automate complex system tasks, going beyond Bash can open up new possibilities for your Unix-based systems. So take the leap, try out these shells, and discover which one suits your needs and style best. Happy shelling!

Chapter 24: Going Beyond Bash: Advanced Shells for the Adventurous

1. **Bash** is undoubtedly the most popular shell for Unix-based systems, and for good reason. It's powerful, versatile, and comes pre-installed on most systems. However, **Bash** is just one of many shells available for interacting with the system. If you're ready to push your shell skills further, there are several other advanced shells that offer unique features, improved performance, and additional functionalities for those who crave something more than the standard Bash experience. In this chapter, we'll explore some of these **advanced shells**, examining their distinctive features, advantages, and why they might appeal to the adventurous Unix user.

2. **Zsh (Z Shell)**: One of the most popular alternatives to Bash is **Zsh** (Z Shell). Zsh is known for its impressive feature set, including enhanced tab completion, better history management, and superior scripting capabilities. It offers a more user-friendly experience with better **auto-completion**, **globbing**, and **pattern matching**.

    One of Zsh's standout features is its **interactive features**. For example, Zsh has **advanced tab completion**, which can complete not just file names but also command options, function names, and more. If you type a command and press `Tab`, Zsh will offer suggestions for completing the command based on context.

    Zsh also allows you to **customize the prompt** in more interesting ways than Bash. With Zsh, you can easily add information about the current git branch, the status of your last command, or your system's performance metrics right into the prompt.

    To install Zsh:

    ```bash
    ```
    Copy

    ```bash
    sudo apt install zsh
    ```

3.

    After installation, you can change your default shell to Zsh using:

    ```bash
    ```
    Copy

    ```bash
    chsh -s $(which zsh)
    ```

4.

    Zsh is often the preferred choice for users who want a more feature-rich interactive shell experience and for those who appreciate a highly customizable environment.

5. **Fish (Friendly Interactive Shell)**: If you're looking for a shell that combines the ease of use with powerful features, **Fish** is an excellent choice. Fish is designed to be simple and user-friendly, with **automatic suggestions**, **syntax highlighting**, and **easy-to-read error messages**.

    Fish's standout feature is its **autosuggestions**. As you type, Fish will suggest commands based on your command history or common patterns, making it much faster to execute common tasks. Fish also provides **syntax highlighting**, so if you make a typo or enter a command incorrectly, it will be highlighted in color, making it easy to spot errors in real-time.

    Unlike Zsh and Bash, Fish doesn't rely on **bashrc** or **zshrc** files for customization. Instead, it uses a dedicated configuration file that is more user-friendly, with commands written in Fish's own scripting language.

To install Fish:
bash
Copy

```
sudo apt install fish
```

6.

To change your default shell to Fish:
bash
Copy

```
chsh -s $(which fish)
```

7.

Fish is a great shell for beginners who want powerful features out of the box without the need for heavy configuration or scripting knowledge.

8. **Tcsh (TENEX C Shell):** Tcsh is a variant of the original **C shell (csh)** and is known for its **command-line editing** and **file name completion** features. Tcsh offers a **C-like syntax**, which may appeal to users who are familiar with programming languages like C or Java. While it is not as widely used as Zsh or Bash, it has a loyal user base that appreciates its syntax and advanced features.

   Some of Tcsh's features include **command history**, **customizable prompts**, and the ability to **work with a variety of wildcard characters** for file completion. It also includes a unique feature called **aliasing**, which allows you to define new commands or shortcuts for frequent tasks.

   To install Tcsh:
   bash
   Copy

```
sudo apt install tcsh
```

9.

Tcsh is a good choice for users who prefer the C shell's syntax and want a customizable, efficient interactive shell experience.

10. **Ksh (KornShell):** **Ksh** is an advanced shell that combines the features of the Bourne shell (`sh`) with additional features for scripting, making it a powerful tool for users who need to write complex scripts. Ksh offers better performance for large-scale scripts than some other shells, and its scripting features make it ideal for system administrators. Ksh has built-in support for **command history**, **job control**, **pattern matching**, and **scripting functions**. One of its most notable features is its **brace expansion** and **command substitution**, which allow for complex operations to be done more easily. For example, Ksh provides a shorthand for creating lists of files or iterating over a set of items.

    To install Ksh:

    bash
    Copy

```
sudo apt install ksh
```

11.

    Ksh is best suited for users who prefer a scripting environment that's more consistent with traditional Unix shells but still offers advanced features for automation and scripting.

12. **Dash (Debian Almquist Shell):** If you need a **lightweight shell** that's optimized for performance and used primarily for scripting, **Dash** is an excellent choice. Dash is often the default shell for **system scripts** on Debian-based distributions, including Ubuntu. It's designed to be **fast** and **minimalistic**, so if you're working on scripts where performance is critical, Dash might be the shell for you.

    Dash is a POSIX-compliant shell, which means it sticks closely to the specifications of the **POSIX shell** standard. While it may not offer as many interactive features as Zsh or Fish, Dash's focus is on executing scripts quickly and efficiently, making it ideal for system-level tasks.

    Dash is usually pre-installed on many systems, but you can switch to it if you prefer:

    bash
    Copy

```
sudo chsh -s /bin/dash
```

13.

    Dash is a great choice for scripting, especially if you need to optimize for speed and compatibility with POSIX standards.

14. **Sh (Bourne Shell)**: The **Bourne shell (sh)** is the oldest and most basic Unix shell. While it doesn't have many of the features of more modern shells like Bash or Zsh, it's still commonly used for system scripts due to its **POSIX compliance** and simplicity. Most of the basic shell scripting techniques can be accomplished in `sh`, but modern features like interactive command completion, advanced tab expansion, and rich syntax are not available.

    Despite its simplicity, **sh** remains an essential tool for writing scripts that need to run across different Unix-like systems, as it has very few dependencies.

15. **Advanced Shell Customization**: Many of these advanced shells provide powerful customization options, allowing you to tailor your environment to suit your needs. Whether it's tweaking your prompt with Zsh, adding aliases in Fish, or adjusting the file completion rules in Tcsh, customizing your shell environment can dramatically increase your productivity.

    For example, in **Zsh**, you can change your prompt to display the current directory and git branch by editing your `.zshrc` file:

    bash
    Copy

```
PROMPT='%~ %(!.#.>)'   # Displays the current directory
and a prompt that changes based on user privileges.
```

16.

    Similarly, Fish makes it easy to customize the shell environment by modifying its configuration file (`~/.config/fish/config.fish`). You can set environment variables, change prompt styles, and more, all without writing complex configuration scripts.

    Exploring the advanced features of each shell and experimenting with different customizations can help you create an efficient and personalized terminal environment.

17. **Choosing the Right Shell**: Each of the shells we've discussed has its own set of strengths, and choosing the right shell often depends on your specific needs and preferences. Here are some guidelines to help you choose:

    o   Choose **Zsh** if you want a feature-rich shell with powerful tab completion, customization, and advanced scripting support.

    o   Opt for **Fish** if you prefer an easy-to-use, interactive shell with auto-suggestions and syntax highlighting, perfect for beginners and those who want a modern shell experience.

    o   **Tcsh** is best for those who prefer C-like syntax or are coming from a C programming background.

- o **Ksh** is ideal for users who need a powerful, POSIX-compliant scripting shell for complex tasks and high-performance scripts.

- o **Dash** is perfect for system scripts where speed and minimal resource usage are crucial.

- o Stick with **sh** if you need simplicity and POSIX compliance across different systems.

18. **In conclusion**, Bash is an excellent shell, but there's a whole world of other shells out there to explore. From Zsh's customizability and Fish's user-friendly features to the speed of Dash and the power of Ksh, these advanced shells can help you work smarter, faster, and more efficiently. Whether you're looking to optimize your interactive experience or automate complex system tasks, going beyond Bash can open up new possibilities for your Unix-based systems. So take the leap, try out these shells, and discover which one suits your needs and style best. Happy shelling!

Cross-Shell Script Compatibility: As you dive into different shells, you may encounter situations where you need your scripts to work seamlessly across multiple shell environments. While many shells follow **POSIX standards** for basic scripting, there are unique features and syntax differences between them. Ensuring cross-shell compatibility can be a challenge, but with a few best practices, you can write scripts that run smoothly across various shells.

- **Stick to POSIX-compliant features**: When writing scripts that should work on multiple shells, it's essential to adhere to POSIX standards. Avoid shell-specific features that may not be supported in all shells, such as Zsh's advanced tab completion or Fish's unique syntax.

- **Use the correct shebang**: Always start your script with a **shebang** line to specify the shell in which the script should run. For example:

```
bash
Copy
```

```
#!/bin/bash   # For a script that should run in Bash
```

- ```
  #!/bin/zsh   # For a script that should run in Zsh
  ```
-

- **Test across shells**: Before deploying a script, make sure it runs as expected in the shells it's intended for. Tools like **shellcheck** can help identify potential issues and provide suggestions for making your script more portable.

By keeping these practices in mind, you can ensure your scripts work smoothly across multiple shell environments, making them more flexible and portable.
  ```

The Future of Shells: Shells have come a long way since their inception, and as the Unix ecosystem continues to evolve, so too do the tools we use to interact with it. New features, such as better integration with cloud services, enhanced security protocols, and further automation capabilities, are constantly being developed. The rise of **containerized environments** (like Docker) and **serverless architectures** has led to more sophisticated, lightweight, and purpose-built shells to cater to modern use cases.

- **Cloud-based shells**: With the increasing reliance on cloud services, shells that can integrate directly with cloud environments, such as **AWS CloudShell** or **Google Cloud Shell**, are becoming more popular. These shells allow developers to manage their cloud infrastructure without needing to switch between multiple tools.

- **AI-powered shells**: Looking ahead, there's potential for **AI-powered shell environments** that can assist with automation, error correction, and smart recommendations, further streamlining workflows.

The future of shells will likely revolve around integrating these new tools into traditional shell environments while maintaining the flexibility and power that have made shells an essential part of Unix-based systems.

Learning and Experimenting with New Shells: As you continue your journey with Unix-like systems, one of the most important skills is learning how to adapt to new tools and environments. Just as you may have started with Bash and gradually explored other shells like Zsh, Fish, and Ksh, keep an open mind and experiment with emerging shells. Each one offers unique capabilities that can improve your workflow and help you solve problems more efficiently.

Consider **setting up virtual environments** for testing and exploring new shells. For example, using **Docker** or **Vagrant** can provide isolated environments where you can try different shells and configurations without worrying about affecting your main system. This experimentation process allows you to continuously improve your shell skills and stay ahead of the curve.

In Conclusion, the world of Unix shells is vast, with a variety of options tailored to different needs. While **Bash** will always be a staple in the Unix world, exploring shells like **Zsh**, **Fish**, **Ksh**, and others opens up a world of possibilities, allowing you to enhance your productivity, streamline your workflows, and tailor your environment to suit your personal preferences.

Each shell brings something unique to the table, whether it's improved interactivity, faster scripting performance, or more advanced automation capabilities. By experimenting with these shells, understanding their strengths, and customizing your environment, you'll gain deeper insights into how Unix systems work and become more efficient in your daily tasks.

So go ahead—venture beyond Bash. Try out Zsh's customization options, explore Fish's intuitive features, or dive into the power of Ksh scripting. The more you explore, the more powerful your Unix toolkit becomes. Happy shell exploration!

Chapter 25: Becoming a Unix Rockstar: Commands, Tools, and Tips You'll Love

1. **Becoming a Unix Rockstar** isn't just about knowing a handful of commands or understanding how the filesystem works. It's about mastering the tools and tips that make working with Unix faster, smoother, and more enjoyable. Whether you're a beginner or an experienced user, there are always new tricks and tools to discover that will enhance your workflow. In this chapter, we'll dive into some of the coolest, most useful commands and tools in the Unix ecosystem, as well as some tips and tricks that will make you feel like a Unix rockstar in no time.

2. **The Mighty `grep`**: One of the first commands every Unix user should master is **`grep`**. It's the Swiss army knife of text searching and is incredibly powerful when combined with other commands. `grep` searches through text files for patterns, making it indispensable for log analysis, text processing, or just finding specific strings within files. For example, to search for the word "error" in a log file:
   bash
   Copy

   ```
   grep "error" /var/log/syslog
   ```

3.

   You can use **regular expressions** to make `grep` even more powerful. For example, to find lines starting with "error" or "fail," you could use:
   bash
   Copy

   ```
   grep -E "^(error|fail)" /var/log/syslog
   ```

4.

   `grep` can also show you the line number where the match is found:
   bash
   Copy

   ```
   grep -n "error" /var/log/syslog
   ```

5.

   Mastering `grep` is like unlocking a secret weapon for any text-based search task.

6. **The Power of awk**: If you're not familiar with **awk**, you're missing out on one of the most powerful text-processing tools available in Unix. awk allows you to perform complex operations on data, such as splitting columns, performing calculations, and even modifying content in files.

    For example, let's say you have a CSV file and want to print the first column:

    bash
    Copy

    ```
    awk -F, '{print $1}' data.csv
    ```

7. You can also use awk to sum a column of numbers:

    bash
    Copy

    ```
    awk '{sum += $1} END {print sum}' numbers.txt
    ```

8. awk can even perform pattern matching and conditional actions, which makes it an essential tool for anyone working with structured text or logs.

9. **sed—Stream Editor for Transformations**: **sed** is another indispensable tool that every Unix user should be familiar with. It's a stream editor that allows you to perform basic text transformations on an input stream (like a file or a pipeline). It's perfect for automated editing, replacing patterns, or transforming files.

    A basic example of using sed to replace text:

    bash
    Copy

    ```
    sed 's/old_text/new_text/g' file.txt
    ```

10. The **s** stands for substitute, and **g** means global (replace all occurrences). You can also use sed to delete lines matching a pattern:

```bash
Copy
```

```
sed '/pattern/d' file.txt
```

11.

sed is incredibly powerful for making changes to files or streams, especially when combined with pipes.

12. The Humble `find` Command: The `find` command is your go-to tool for locating files and directories on your system. It's ideal for searching files by name, type, size, modification time, and other criteria. The power of `find` comes from its flexibility and the ability to perform actions on the files it locates.

To find all `.txt` files in a directory and its subdirectories:

```bash
Copy
```

```
find /path/to/directory -name "*.txt"
```

13.

You can also run commands on the files `find` locates. For example, to delete all `.bak` files:

```bash
Copy
```

```
find /path/to/directory -name "*.bak" -exec rm {} \;
```

14.

The `-exec` flag allows you to execute commands on the files that `find` returns, making it a powerful tool for managing large file systems.

15. `tmux`—Terminal Multiplexer: If you've ever wished you could split your terminal into multiple panes, work with multiple tabs, or even keep your session running after disconnecting, **`tmux`** is the tool for you. `tmux` is a terminal multiplexer that allows you to manage multiple terminal windows from a single screen.

With `tmux`, you can split your terminal into panes, switch between sessions, and keep processes running even when you disconnect from the terminal. For example, to create a new tmux session:

bash
Copy

```
tmux new-session -s mysession
```

16.

To split the window vertically:

bash
Copy

```
Ctrl+b %   # Press Ctrl+b, then % for vertical split
```

17.

tmux can transform your productivity by allowing you to multitask within a single terminal window. You can even use **tmux** over SSH to keep long-running processes alive when you disconnect.

18. **xargs—The Command-Line Helper**: **xargs** is a command-line tool that takes input from standard input and converts it into arguments for other commands. This is particularly useful when working with commands that don't accept input directly from a pipe.

For example, to delete all .log files in a directory:

bash
Copy

```
find . -name "*.log" | xargs rm
```

19.

In this case, xargs takes the list of files output by find and passes them as arguments to the rm command, deleting them all at once. This can be a game-changer when dealing with large numbers of files.

20. **htop—A More Interactive Task Manager**: If you're tired of the traditional, text-based top command, **htop** is a more interactive and user-friendly alternative. htop provides

a dynamic, real-time view of your system's processes, CPU usage, memory usage, and other statistics.

With htop, you can scroll through processes, search for specific tasks, and even kill or send signals to processes directly from the interface. It's perfect for anyone who needs a more visual, hands-on approach to monitoring system performance.

To install htop:

bash
Copy

```
sudo apt install htop
```

21.

Once installed, simply type htop in the terminal, and enjoy a more interactive and detailed process view.

22. curl and wget — Downloading Files from the Web: curl and **wget** are two powerful commands that let you download files from the internet. They're particularly useful for automating downloads, interacting with APIs, and fetching data from web servers.

- To download a file with wget:
  bash
  Copy

  ```
  wget http://example.com/file.zip
  ```

-

- To download a file with curl:
  bash
  Copy

  ```
  curl -O http://example.com/file.zip
  ```

-

23. While `wget` is excellent for downloading entire directories or recursively downloading content, `curl` is more versatile and widely used for making HTTP requests to interact with APIs, download data, and more.

24. `rsync`—**Efficient File Synchronization**: `rsync` is a powerful tool for syncing files and directories between local and remote systems. It's incredibly efficient because it only transfers the changes (differences) between source and destination, making it perfect for backups, mirroring, and system administration.
To sync a directory to a remote system:
bash
Copy

```
rsync -avz /path/to/source/ user@remote:/path/to/
destination/
```

25.

The `-a` flag preserves file permissions and timestamps, `-v` enables verbose output, and `-z` compresses the data during transfer. `rsync` is an essential tool for system administrators and anyone who needs to keep files synchronized across multiple locations.

26. The Magic of `alias`: One of the quickest ways to boost your efficiency on the command line is by creating **aliases** for your most frequently used commands. Aliases let you assign shorter or more memorable names to long commands or command sequences. For example, instead of typing `ls -la` every time you want to list files with details, you can create an alias:
bash
Copy

```
alias ll='ls -la'
```

27.

This alias makes the command `ll` equivalent to `ls -la`, saving you keystrokes and streamlining your workflow. Aliases can be added to your `.bashrc` or `.zshrc` files for persistence across sessions.

28. In Conclusion, becoming a Unix Rockstar involves not just learning commands, but also discovering the **tools** and **tricks** that help you work smarter. The commands, tools, and tips we've covered in this chapter are just the tip of the iceberg—Unix is a vast world of possibilities, and with the right tools, you can handle any task with confidence and efficiency. By mastering these tools and incorporating them into your daily workflow, you'll soon be navigating your Unix-based system like a true pro. Keep exploring, keep learning, and you'll continue to level up your Unix skills. Happy rockstar-ing!

Mastering Keyboard Shortcuts: To truly elevate your Unix game, learning **keyboard shortcuts** is essential. These shortcuts can dramatically speed up your work in the terminal, allowing you to navigate, manipulate text, and control processes with minimal effort. Here are some of the most useful keyboard shortcuts in Unix:

- **Ctrl+C**: Stop a running command or process.

- **Ctrl+Z**: Suspend a process and send it to the background.

- **Ctrl+D**: Exit the terminal or close a shell session.

- **Ctrl+L**: Clear the screen, giving you a fresh view of the terminal.

- **Ctrl+A**: Move the cursor to the beginning of the line.

- **Ctrl+E**: Move the cursor to the end of the line.

- **Ctrl+U**: Delete everything before the cursor on the current line.

- **Ctrl+K**: Delete everything after the cursor on the current line.

- **Ctrl+W**: Delete the word before the cursor.

- **Tab**: Auto-complete file and command names, making navigation faster.

Mastering these shortcuts can save you time and make using the terminal more efficient, allowing you to focus on the tasks at hand.

System Monitoring Tools: As a Unix Rockstar, it's important to have the right tools for monitoring system performance. Whether you're tracking CPU usage, memory usage, or disk space, these tools provide valuable insights into the health of your system.

- **top**: Displays real-time information about running processes, including CPU and memory usage.

bash
Copy

```
top
```

- **free**: Shows the system's memory usage, including free and used memory.

bash
Copy

```
free -h
```
- **df**: Displays disk space usage for your system's file systems.

bash
Copy
```
df -h
```
- **iotop**: Shows real-time disk I/O usage by processes, useful for diagnosing performance bottlenecks.

bash
Copy
```
sudo apt install iotop
sudo iotop
```
These monitoring tools are indispensable for keeping an eye on your system's performance and ensuring it operates efficiently.

The Power of find and xargs: The combination of **find** and **xargs** is one of the most powerful and versatile techniques in Unix. It allows you to search for files and then apply commands to them. For example, you can use **find** to locate all **.log** files and then delete them with **xargs**:

bash
Copy
```
find /path/to/directory -name "*.log" | xargs rm
```
This example finds all **.log** files and uses **xargs** to pass them to the **rm** command, which deletes them. This method is efficient and allows you to apply any command to the files found by **find**.

Job Control and Background Processing: As a Unix Rockstar, knowing how to manage processes is crucial for multitasking and improving efficiency. Using **background processing** and **job control** commands allows you to run multiple tasks at once without cluttering up your terminal.

- **&**: Run a command in the background.

bash
Copy
```
long_running_command &
```
- **jobs**: List background jobs.

bash
Copy
```
jobs
```
- **fg**: Bring a background job to the foreground.

```bash
Copy
fg %1
```

- **bg**: Resume a suspended job in the background.

```bash
Copy
bg %1
```

By mastering job control, you can keep your terminal clean and manage multiple tasks simultaneously, improving your productivity and making it easier to work with long-running processes.

Working with Permissions and Ownership: One of the key features of Unix-based systems is the ability to control access to files and directories. Learning how to manage **file permissions** and **ownership** will ensure that your system is secure and properly configured.

- **chmod**: Change file permissions. For example, to make a file executable:

```bash
Copy
chmod +x script.sh
```

- **chown**: Change file ownership. To change the owner of a file:

```bash
Copy
sudo chown user:user file.txt
```

- **chgrp**: Change the group ownership of a file.

```bash
Copy
sudo chgrp group file.txt
```

Mastering these commands will help you secure your files and control who has access to them.

Compression and Archiving: Dealing with large amounts of data? **Compression and archiving** tools will save space and make file management easier. The most common tools are `tar`, `gzip`, and `zip`, each of which has different use cases.

- **tar**: Archive files and directories. To create a `.tar` archive:

```bash
Copy
tar -cvf archive.tar /path/to/files
```

To extract the contents of a `.tar` archive:

```bash
```

```
tar -xvf archive.tar
```

- **gzip**: Compress files using the **gzip** format.

bash
```
gzip file.txt
```

- **zip**: Compress files into a `.zip` archive.

bash
```
zip archive.zip file1.txt file2.txt
```

Compression and archiving tools allow you to manage large datasets and backup your files efficiently.

Creating Aliases for Efficiency: One of the easiest ways to boost productivity in the terminal is by using **aliases**. Aliases allow you to create shortcuts for commands you frequently use, saving you time and effort.

For example, to create an alias for listing files in a detailed view:

bash
```
alias ll='ls -la'
```

You can also create complex aliases for frequently used multi-command sequences:

bash
```
alias update='sudo apt update && sudo apt upgrade -y'
```

Adding these aliases to your `.bashrc` or `.zshrc` file will ensure they're available every time you open a new terminal session.

In Conclusion, becoming a Unix Rockstar isn't just about memorizing commands—it's about learning how to **work smarter** and use the full power of the Unix ecosystem. The tools and tips covered in this chapter, from `grep` and `awk` to `tmux` and `xargs`, will help you streamline your workflow, automate repetitive tasks, and manage your system more effectively. As you continue exploring the rich world of Unix, keep experimenting with new commands, exploring hidden gems, and building your toolkit. Soon, you'll be tackling complex tasks with ease, impressing your peers with your Unix mastery. Keep rocking the command line!